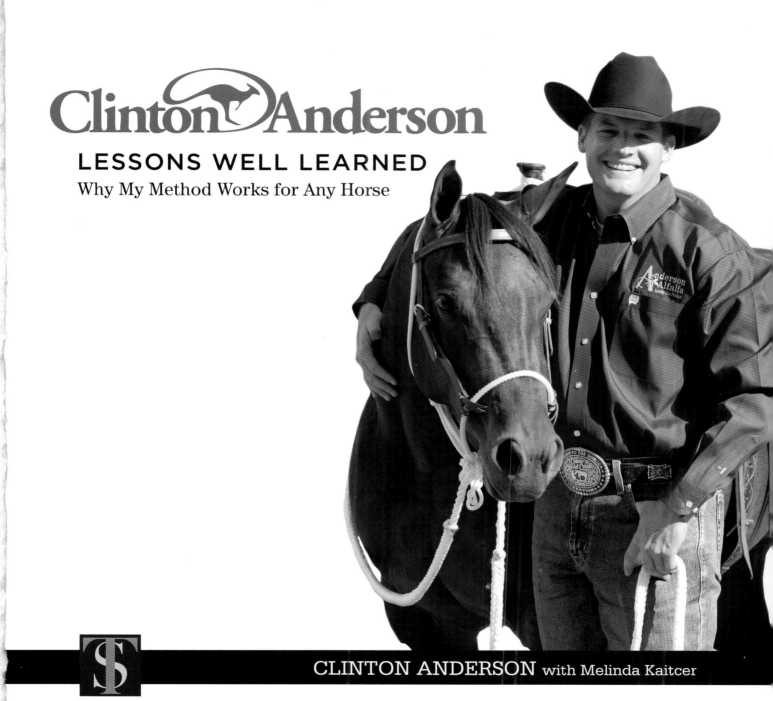

Clinton Anderson

LESSONS WELL LEARNED

Why My Method Works for Any Horse

CLINTON ANDERSON with Melinda Kaitcer

First published in 2009 by
Trafalgar Square Books
North Pomfret, Vermont 05053

Printed in China

Copyright © 2009 Clinton Anderson

Disclaimer of Liability
The authors and publisher shall have neither liability nor responsibility to any person or entity with respect to any loss or damage caused or alleged to be caused directly or indirectly by the information contained in this book. While the book is as accurate as the authors can make it, there may be errors, omissions, and inaccuracies.

The authors have made very effort to obtain a release from all persons pictured in the photographs used in this book. In some cases, however, the persons may not have been known and therefore could not be contacted.

Library of Congress Cataloging-in-Publication Data

Anderson, Clinton.
  [Lessons well learned]
  Clinton Anderson's Lessons well learned : why my method works for any horse / Clinton Anderson with Melinda Kaitcer.
    p. cm.
  Includes index.
  ISBN 978-1-57076-435-6
  1. Horses--Training. I. Kaitcer, Melinda. II. Title. III. Title: Lessons well learned.
  SF287.A575 2009
  636.1'0835--dc22
                                  2009031048

Photos courtesy of Clinton Anderson

WARNING

Equine training can be a hazardous activity, which may subject the participants to possible serious injury. Clinton Anderson and his associates will not assume any liability for your actions.

This book provides general information, instructions, and techniques that may not be suitable for everyone. No warranty is given regarding the suitability of this information, the instructions, and techniques to you or other individuals acting under your directions. Personal instruction, in addition to viewing Clinton Anderson's entire equine video series, is suggested to best understand these training ideas.

Book and jacket designed by Carrie Fradkin
Book cover designed by Stewart & Associates, Louisville, KY
Typefaces: ITC Century, Serifa

10 9 8 7 6

"What drives me is trying to be the best horseman I can be and helping people form better relationships with their horses. I am here to give them everything I've got."

Clinton Anderson—"Inspiring the Dreams of Horsemen"

Contents

INTRODUCTION

From Downunder to Here

A lifelong passion begins

I can't remember a time in my life when I haven't been drawn to horses. But like many of you, I wasn't born into the life I lead today. I grew up in Australia where my family lived in the city. My sister and I lived for the weekends when we could visit my grandparents' farm, and it was there that my lifelong passion for working with horses began. Some of my earliest horse memories are of the velvet softness of my grandmother's horse's nose and of being led around the paddock on her horse's back. Even though she didn't know a whole lot about horsemanship, she really encouraged our interest in horses, and she was always trying to learn more. When I was nine, my grandparents bought me my first horse, a belligerent mare named Casey, who to this day remains one of the pushiest, most disrespectful horses I've ever known.

Because at the time I had no idea about training or equipment, I was all about quick fixes. My grandfather and I once put a running martingale on Casey in such a way that I later learned could have caused her to flip over backward and maybe have crushed me to death. But I got lucky. I like to tell this story because I think a lot of people assume I started with all the knowledge I have today. Quite the contrary, in the beginning I didn't know anything about what I was doing. So if you think I can't relate to where you are when you're starting out with horses, let's set the record straight: I definitely can.

Picking up speed

My horsemanship skills first began to grow because of my obsession with a popular equestrian sport in Australia called polocrosse—a fast-paced combination of polo and lacrosse. As a young boy, I lived near a local polocrosse club and it was there that my fascination soon turned to participation. I sold Casey and my parents bought my first polocrosse horse, Bess, for $1,000. By today's standards, she really wasn't much, but we thought she was the greatest thing in the world. From age 12 to 15, I ate, slept, and breathed polocrosse. It's all I wanted to do, and I practiced all the time. But I quickly discovered that I needed to know more.

While my teammates and I were all good riders, as far as having good balance and an independent seat (we had to or we would have been killed playing the game), we didn't have any horsemanship skills. Our horses were also very poorly trained—they couldn't stop, turn, or back up with any consistency. And, as you can probably imagine, since polocrosse is an intense game with a lot of galloping, these horses were also pretty high-spirited. Nevertheless, the last year I played polocrosse, I qualified for an Australian national junior polocrosse team and Bess was named Jr. Horse of the Year.

Learning the ropes

When I was 13, a man watching our polocrosse match told my father about a horse trainer and clinician from Rockhampton named Gordon McKinlay who could probably help me with my horsemanship skills. Although I was always drawn to communicating with my horse and had eagerly absorbed any information on horses that I could find, I wasn't having a whole lot of success putting it to use. When I heard that there was a man who could help me with this, I jumped at the opportunity.

My mother and my grandparents drove nearly 20 hours to take me to Longreach, Queensland, so I could participate in Gordon McKinlay's clinic. This was my first exposure to the training techniques that made a world of difference to me and to my horse—very similar to the exercises that have now become part of my method for gaining control of a horse's feet in order to earn his respect. One of the best exercises he taught me, the *One-Rein Stop*, made such a difference in my ability to rate Bess's speed and get her to stop I was absolutely amazed.

Before that clinic, I never realized that you could actually get paid to train a horse. Making a living from training horses, I thought, had to be the greatest deal in the world. After that clinic, I was determined to become a horse trainer, and I was willing to do everything in my power to reach my goal. Not only did I want to be a horse trainer, but I wanted to be the very best one I could be, and I knew that Gordon McKinlay could help me. When Gordon invited me to come to his ranch to work with him on school holidays, I, of course, took him up on his offer.

As I began practicing at home what I had learned at the clinic, little by little, Bess and I got better and better. People began noticing how I could back her up, stop her and do quick turns, and I started having opportunities to train horses for other kids in the area. By the time I was 14 and in the tenth grade, I had trained two horses, charging $50 a week each. On top of this, I pushed trolleys (shopping carts) two afternoons a week at a local Kmart®. That job paid me $80. So when I was in high school, I was making $180 a week, which was quite a bit back then. From a very early age, my parents taught me that if I wanted something, I had to save up my money and buy it for myself. I discovered in the process that I loved working hard, reaping the rewards, and enjoying the satisfaction of knowing that I had earned the money myself.

It was about this time that Gordon offered me a permanent position as his apprentice, and there was nothing I wanted more in the world. In Australia, it's mandatory to stay in school until you're 15 years of age. After 15, it's optional whether or not you complete grades 11 and 12. When I told my parents that I was going to leave school and go to work for Gordon, as you might imagine, I met a lot of resistance. But when it came down to it, my parents supported my decision.

Although that may sound somewhat odd, my parents realized two things. First, I was talented at training horses and I loved it. Second, they knew that if you can find something you're passionate about and something you're good at in life, you had better head down that track. I suppose they also knew that if they made me stay in school, I was going to make their life miserable for the next two years!

When I broke the news that I planned to leave school to everyone else—my guidance counselor, my teachers, my friends, and family members—they were against it. Everybody thought I was making the biggest mistake of my life. They couldn't understand how I could make a living from training horses. I can remember taking horse magazines from the United States to my guidance counselor and saying, "Look, people make a living out of this. This is not just a hobby. It's an actual business."

Of course, when I decided to leave school, it helped that my parents knew Gordon's place was safe and I couldn't get into any trouble. He lived out in the middle of nowhere, and I worked seven days a week for two years. It didn't bother me that there weren't any days off, because I absolutely loved what I was doing. Not only did I work seven days a week, but I worked only for room and board—Gordon never paid me a cent. I was lucky enough to have parents who gave me a little bit of money for food and clothes, but I didn't need much of anything. I didn't have a car, I didn't have a girlfriend, and I certainly didn't have a social life. My whole life revolved around learning from Gordon and working horses for him.

My apprenticeship wasn't just about horse training. He baled hay year round, and I was in the field working right beside him. More than once I stacked 3,000 bales of hay by myself. I slaughtered cattle and sheep, built and painted fences, cleaned stalls—whatever needed to be done. Gordon taught me a lot of great life lessons, but the most important one he taught me was when you get into trouble, learn from it, put a smile on your face, and move on. To this day, what I learned helps me acknowledge criticism, accept it, learn from it, and then move on. My time with Gordon built my character and helped shape me into the person I am today.

Reining, cutting, and cow horses

After two years, I had a great foundation in horsemanship skills, but I wanted to learn more about the reining, cutting, and cow horse industries. Building on what I learned from Gordon, I went to work for Ian Francis, the three-time Australian National Cutting Horse Association Futurity Champion and five-time Australian National Reining Horse Association Futurity Champion. Growing up, I had watched Ian at horse shows and was amazed at what he could do with a horse. His ability to ride and show a horse was above and beyond anyone else's at the time. I knew that an apprenticeship under him would take my horsemanship to another level.

I studied with Ian for a year and every hour I was out there training a horse, I was learning something. Unlike a lot of top trainers who only tell half the story for fear of giving away their secrets, Ian was never afraid to share his knowledge with me. Of course, I asked him nearly a hundred questions a day and made it nearly impossible for him to ignore me, but he freely shared his training methods, and I still practice those same techniques on my own horses today. In fact, I still continue to learn from Ian, and I try to fly him over to the United States at least once a year to continue building my knowledge. Every time I watch Ian ride, I always learn something new; he still never fails to amaze me.

While the most important thing Gordon taught me was how to be safe while working with horses, what Ian showed me was his ability to get a horse soft and supple. I often say that Ian can make a hollow log look like a *broke* hollow log. As I had hoped, the feel and timing I developed under Gordon got increasingly better riding with Ian. His unique ability to see things from a horse's perspective makes him the best at getting a young horse to do things without force. He can make a horse of even the most average ability do things that make you say, "Wow."

At the end of my apprenticeship with Ian, I felt confident in my ability to not only start a colt and handle problem horses, but I had also developed the feel, timing, and experience to prepare a horse to show. Although lot of trainers can start colts, it takes a lot more to get a horse soft enough and broke enough to compete and win at national shows.

My own place at last

With my parents' help, I left Ian's to open my own 66-acre training barn in Rockhampton. Starting out, I didn't have enough money to pay someone to help me, so I did all the work myself. I trained the horses, I cleaned the stalls, I saddled the horses and unsaddled them. I held horses for the vet, I fed them, I trimmed hooves—you name it, I did it. For the first couple of years after I went out on my own, I didn't turn any horses away no matter what their problem. If someone brought me an eight-year-old, wild-eyed brumby (the free-roaming feral horses in Australia) to break in, I'd smile and say, "I'd love to."

Working with all those problem horses helped me develop my training skills and prepared me for being able to handle any horse. For the most part, I kept each horse I trained for just six weeks. At the end of that time, the owner would come and pick the horse up. If I did happen to get a nice show horse to train, I'd get to ride him for 60 to 90 days and then the owner would come, take him home and show him. I soon realized that the only way I was going to get to prove myself in the show arena was to own my own horse.

When I first saw a photo of Mindy in *Australian Quarter Horse Magazine*, she was just two months old. I was instantly drawn to her looks, her style, and her breeding. My gut told me there was something special about this horse. Mindy's $3,000 price tag was a huge gamble for a starving horse trainer but with my parents' help, I scraped up the money. It was one of the best decisions I ever made.

Something else happened when owners came to pick up their horse after training. I'd always show them what the horse could do, then after I rode the horse, I'd give them a 20- to 30-minute lesson to show them how to control their horse at home. At the end of these lessons, most people would say, "Clinton, I really enjoyed the lesson, and I really liked the way you explained the information to me, but there's no way I'm going to remember everything we just covered. Can I come back in a couple of weeks and have you give me another lesson?"

I'd say, "Sure, bring him back," because I could always use the money. These customers started telling their friends about me and pretty soon, they'd show up with their friends and ask if I could give them lessons, too. Then they'd call and say they had seven neighbors interested in getting lessons—and could I go to them instead? That was the start of my mini-clinics, and little did I know it would lead to the horsemanship clinics and teaching that would eventually consume my life.

As this part of my business continued to grow, I remembered something Gordon told me. He'd say, "Clinton, there aren't enough hours in the day to make good money with your own two hands. You've got to be able to duplicate yourself as many times as you can." Ian, too, had echoed this thought with his own piece of advice: "Clinton, you can only ride so many horses in a day."

The last year I was in Australia I worked 10 horses a day in addition to giving lessons and mini-clinics. My days started at five in the morning and, if I was lucky, I was done by nine or 10 in the evening. I loved what I did for a living, but I was starting to realize that training horses offered a limited income. Following Gordon's advice to duplicate myself and my teaching methods, I decided to make instructional videotapes.

I hired a television crew from a local news station, and I made three videos: *Trouble-Free Trailering, Suppleness and Body Collection,* and *Maneuvers.* I wrote all of my training exercises down on a piece of paper, stuck the paper in my pocket, and just let the cameras roll. After each exercise, I pulled the paper out, read it, and then stuck it back in my pocket and went on to the next one. Mindy was the star of the videos, and I looked like a 12-year-old kid, but ironically, these videos were actually pretty good for the time that they were done.

Gathering knowledge stateside

After my apprenticeship with Ian, I really wanted to get involved in the reining and cutting worlds. Ian had taught me how to put the finishing touches on a show horse and how to prepare a horse to compete, but I still wanted more knowledge. In 1995, Sam Smith, a reining trainer from Ohio, came over to Australia and judged the NRHA (National Reining Horse Association) Futurity. I got to talking with him and when I was 21, I came to the United States to ride with Sam and pick up as much knowledge as I possibly could. While the information I learned was extremely helpful, it turned out that I picked the wrong six months to visit Ohio. Being from north Queensland where temperatures never dip below freezing, the cold Ohio winter was more than I had bargained for. So I thanked Sam for his help and went down to Arizona to ride with multiple NRHA futurity winner, Al Dunning.

Back to Australia

By the time I left the United States to go back to Australia all I really wanted to do was ride Mindy and keep a couple of personal horses to show and compete. I was burned out training horses for others, so to make ends meet, I decided to get a regular day job. But what could I do? I didn't know how to turn a computer on, I couldn't fix anything, I wasn't particularly handy, so I figured the only thing I could do was pump gas. And, after work, I could train my own horses. I knew that I was only going to spend a year in Australia, so this was just a temporary fix.

This turned out to be a lot harder than I expected. Nobody would hire me. This was the first time I realized the risk I had taken by leaving school early. I went around to all the local gas stations trying to find a job. I offered to work the first week for free to prove myself, but people couldn't seem to comprehend that somebody would actually work for free for a chance to have a job. That was the first time in my life I remember getting depressed about my future, but I refused to give up. Finally, I walked into Sizzler® restaurant, found the manager and said, "Listen, I don't care if I have to mop the floors or clean the toilets with a toothbrush, I don't care what I have to do, I will work for free or do whatever I have to do to prove to you that I'm serious and want a job. Will you hire me?"

He did. And for the first six months that I was back in Australia, I worked as a waiter at Sizzler restaurant. Now, I must admit, I was a pretty good waiter. I could clean up dishes and bring food darn well. There's no doubt about that. I worked my horses during the day and went into the restaurant in the evening around 5:00 P.M. and got off at 1:00 A.M. Then, my horse-training clients started to find out I was back. They'd see me in the restaurant, we'd get to talking, and I'd end up agreeing to train a horse for them.

After six months at the Sizzler, I got so busy training horses again that I quit the restaurant and went back to training full time. That experience taught me a very valuable lesson though, and today, I encourage everyone to finish high school and college because it gives you something to fall back on.

Mindy's reining debut

My ultimate goal for Mindy was to take her to the NRHA Futurity in Australia and compete against the top names in the reining world. Although I knew Mindy had the breeding to be a phenomenal reining horse, before I started taking her to futurities and competing, I wanted to make sure I wasn't wasting my efforts. So I sent her to Ian Francis for six weeks, hoping that he could give me a better idea of how much potential she actually had. Ian's verdict was that Mindy was more than capable of being successful at the top of the sport, and he even gave me a couple of tips and pointers to improve her performance.

I look back on this now and realize what great sportsmanship Ian showed by giving me that advice. He did so knowing that I wanted to take Mindy to the Futurity and win—even though he was training a horse for close friends of mine, Bruce and Vicki Neville, to show at the same event.

When I arrived at that Futurity in 1997, I was a 22-year-old nobody had ever heard of—just some kid from the bush. It wasn't until Mindy and I finished our first-go in first place that people started to take notice. Mindy put in her best effort and rode so well that we finished the finals in third place—with just a half a point separating first, second, and third.

From failure arises a new dream

After Mindy did so well in the Futurity, I decided to show reining horses when I got back to the United States. However, even though I had proved myself in Australia with Mindy, getting started in the United States was almost like going back to being an apprentice. I worked for a trainer in Texas and then at a reining barn in California. I actually got fired from that job because the owner's wife didn't like the way I trained horses. I joke about this period of time now and say that these experiences turned out to be the greatest thing that ever happened to me because it was the beginning of Downunder Horsemanship®.

When I started my Downunder Horsemanship company, I had about $400 in the bank, I had just bought a car, and I had no job prospects. The only way I knew to earn enough money was to give as many lessons as I possibly could. I remembered my success with the mini-clinics in Australia and some of the contacts I had made in California seemed keen to learn from me. So I called these people and by word of mouth, I started getting little groups of people together for lessons. From the clinics Gordon and Ian put on, I had a pretty good idea what people liked to get out of them.

In these early days of Downunder Horsemanship clinics, I charged participants $100 a day for a two-day clinic. I might only get three to four people to show up, but one thing led to another, and before I knew it, I had 48 clinics scheduled in my first year. My theory was if I could earn enough money to cover the airfare, I went.

Although I initially started giving clinics as a way to make enough money to buy a good reining horse, my horsemanship clinic business just kept getting bigger and bigger. Before I knew it, I was at a crossroads where I had to choose between training horses and being a teacher. After a couple of years of being a clinician, it was easy to see that there was much more security by going that route, so I made a conscious decision to build Downunder Horsemanship and back off the training.

Even so, I knew even then that it was extremely important to my career to continue to show. Not only did showing help me grow as a horseman—to continually better myself by competing—but staying active in the show world added to my overall credibility. Most other natural horsemanship trainers don't show and, as a result, a lot of horse trainers don't respect them. To this day, I'm about the only clinician who's willing to put his name on the line by going out there and competing.

I kept one or two reining horses that I could have fun on, but I knew that my attention and energy needed to be focused on building my business. If I wanted Downunder Horsemanship to be successful, I had to give it 110 percent. My showing had to take a back seat for quite a few years. I'm still involved in the show world today, but not nearly as much as I would like to be. My main business is still training people and helping them with their horses.

At the first equine exposition I went to, when I was still working in California, I offered to do a general horsemanship session. They were looking for some new, young talent, so they agreed. I talked to maybe 30 or 40 people the entire weekend, but the experience was worth a million bucks because I had time to watch some of the big name clinicians who were there. To be quite honest, although I have the highest respect for them, I looked up in the crowd and saw 2,500 people watching these demonstrations, and thought to myself, "Oh my goodness, you people haven't seen anything yet." I think that was the first time I seriously considered a career as a teacher.

The first thing that I noticed about the top clinicians of that time was their age. Most of them were almost double mine and there was nobody in my age group poised to take over the next generation. So I thought to myself, "Here's a great opportunity, Clinton. At some point, these guys have got to slow down. If you get in there now, by the time they retire, you'll be in the number one position."

If you know my personality, you know that waiting around for someone to retire isn't exactly my style. So it wasn't very long at all before I was nipping at their heels like you wouldn't believe. I watched all the top clinicians, and I said to myself, "I'm going to be better than them in their strengths, and I'm going to avoid their weaknesses."

I think I separated myself from a lot of them mostly by being a "meat-and-potatoes" kind of guy. I'm very black-and-white and "cut to the chase." While you'll never hear me say that my methods are the only correct way—there are a-million-and-one ways to ride and train horses, and there's no one way that's more correct than the other—what you will hear me say is that my program is the easiest, fastest, and safest way to train a horse. I've taken all the guesswork out of training and made it as easy as possible to understand.

In the beginning, my Aussie accent was both a positive and a negative. It was positive in the fact that it was different and people liked to listen to me talk. I think maybe in the beginning, they didn't care whether or not I could teach them—they just liked my accent. The negative was that a lot of people had a hard time understanding me. If you think I have an accent now, it's nothing compared to what it was like when I first came to the United States. In fact, whenever I go back to Australia for a vacation, I've lost so much of my accent that the Australians now have a hard time believing that I'm a native.

Made-for-TV horse training: RFD-TV

In December of 2000, RFD-TV began broadcasting via satellite into millions of homes across America. As the nation's first 24-hour television network dedicated to agriculture and the rural lifestyle, RFD-TV was going into uncharted waters. No one was sure if this new channel would sink or swim, but I decided to take a huge gamble and develop a horse program specifically made for it. This decision turned out to be one of the biggest breaks Downunder Horsemanship could have received.

Unlike the trainers on TV at the time who just chopped their existing videos up and put them on the air, I wanted to give viewers more information than was on my videos. I was the first trainer to take a gamble and purchase my own video equipment. I begged and borrowed every cent I possibly could to do this, which was actually pretty hard for me to do. As a self-employed guy with no tax history in the United States, I didn't have enough credit to buy a pair of underpants from JCPenney™!

Everything that I did with Downunder Horsemanship up until then was completely from cash flow—money I had in my pocket. If RFD-TV had collapsed, I would have gone bankrupt. When I first started my show, I couldn't convince anybody to sponsor me. I'd call up companies and they'd always say, "Who are you?" But I was in it that far, so I had to figure out a way to make it work.

It took a good year for RFD-TV to gain popularity, but once it did, it gave my career a huge boost as far as getting me out in front of a large audience. I've always known that if I could get a crowd in front of me, I could educate them, teach them, and help them, and ultimately, the results would impress them. RFD-TV still puts me in millions of homes across America each week and that exposure has really helped spread the word of Downunder Horsemanship. Call it luck, or call it recognizing a good opportunity and tackling it, RFD-TV put me on the national scene.

"Road to the Horse"

A year after Downunder Horsemanship began broadcasting on TV, an event that showcased the skills of natural horsemanship was begun in Fort Worth, Texas. The show, first called "In a Whisper," but now known as "Road to the Horse," featured three natural horse trainers working with untouched horses. The competition was held over a two-day period and gave contestants just three hours to train their horses to accept a rider and go through an obstacle course.

After years of working with Gordon McKinlay and wild brumbies, I knew I was more than capable of training an unbroken horse to be ridden in three hours. The "Road to the Horse" competition impressed me and became something I wanted to do because it would give the general public a way to compare the abilities of natural horse trainers and clinicians against each other, all in one place. The first year I participated, I competed against Josh Lyons and Curt Pate, two horsemen I greatly respect. Going into the competition, I was the clear underdog. Josh had won the event the year before and Curt was well recognized in the industry.

The one thing that separated me from the other contestants was the amount of time I spent desensitizing and softening my horse. I think it really surprised a lot of people that I was still working with my horse on the ground when the other two were already on their horses. My years of starting colts had taught me the importance of establishing a foundation from the ground before getting on the horse's back. This preparation paid off during the riding portion of the contest. After the freestyle demonstration in which I stood up in the saddle while my horse, a sorrel gelding named Hancock Sug, remained relaxed with his head lowered to the ground, the judges selected me as the winner.

I returned to the competition in 2005 to compete against Craig Cameron and Van Hargis. In the second year, I had to work with Sultry Safari, a gray filly I nicknamed "Precious." If you've ever heard me sarcastically say, "It's all right, Precious," working with this filly is exactly where that phrase came from. She was anything but precious, trying to bite and strike me several times, but my experience working with difficult and belligerent horses helped me convince the filly to work *with* me instead of against me.

Although she was by no means a finished product at the end of the competition, she was sound enough to ride in both directions, navigate an obstacle course, and let me crack a stock whip while standing on her back. Ultimately, we won the event, making me an unprecedented two-time winner of "Road to the Horse." Each time I'm involved with this competition, I try my best to not only win the event, but to educate the audience by demonstrating what's possible if you start a horse's training with a solid foundation.

Taking Downunder Horsemanship
on a United States tour

After my first couple of years teaching Downunder Horsemanship clinics, I decided that the best way to reach as many people as possible would be to tour the country presenting my method in more of a demonstration format. The first tour I did was down in New Mexico, and barely a hundred people showed up. But you know what? I couldn't have been more thrilled. Now, I have my own tractor trailer following me all around the country and 2,500 to 3,000 people usually show at every stop.

People sometimes ask me if I ever dreamed of being famous when I was growing up, and the truth is, no, I didn't. I just wanted to be the best horse trainer I could be. My life has taken a couple of unexpected turns. For example, instead of just training horses, I now spend most of my time training people with the same information I was given. While the fame is a nice part of it, it's not what drives me to do this. What drives me is to be the best horseman I can be and help people understand and form better relationships with their horses.

I'm very thankful for those 3,000 people who show up for my tour stops, screaming, clapping, and cheering me on, and then asking for my autograph, but when I go home, I don't sit and think to myself, "Man, Clinton, you're a big deal." What I do think about is, "People want this information and they've never heard it before—how can I do the best job I can to present it in such a way that they can go home and use it?"

It is in that spirit that I decided to share the lessons I have learned along the way in the form of this book. While I'm still learning every day, I know that the basic principles behind my step-by-step method remain the same. So sit back, mate, relax, and take a walk with me through some of the most valuable lessons I have learned so far and see what you can take with you to build a better relationship and get better results with your horse.

Lesson 1

Frustration ends where knowledge begins

The key to ending frustration and building knowledge, confidence, and ability with horses is a matter of keeping things simple and breaking your goals into specific steps.

SHE

SHE stood in the center of the arena, barking instructions: "Shoulders back, heels down, back straight, eyes up, elbows in, get on the right diagonal, chin up!" As a kid taking English riding lessons back in Australia, I was trying to learn how to post. We circled the arena at a trot, and while I was really just trying my best to stay on the darn horse, my head was spinning with the 20 million things the instructor was asking us to do at once.

This lesson was shaping up like most of the rest of them, leaving me more frustrated than I was when I started. We came to a stop. "Now pull the left rein and when the horse's nose reaches the vertical of the hock, release the rein," she said.

I sat there for a moment, trying my best to figure out what the heck a "vertical" was—and what in the world it had to do with the horse's hock. Finally, I tentatively raised my hand and said, "Let me get this straight. You want me to bend the horse's head with the left rein, and when the horse's nose comes toward my left toe, you want me to release the rein. Is that what you want me to do?"

The instructor looked a little confused, and then she said, "Well, yes, that's exactly what I want you to do."

I thought to myself, "Well, why didn't you just say it like that?"

The lesson I learned in this single, defining moment has stuck with me for the rest of my life—and it turned out to be the first step in my journey to create the method we know today as The Clinton Anderson Method. I think if you ask the majority of people who follow my program

Left: 1.1 **Most of the time when people get frustrated with themselves and their horses, it is because they have run out of knowledge. This young woman is frustrated with a horse that won't back up. Remember: "Frustration begins where knowledge ends."**

1.2 **People like my Method because I make it easy to understand—I keep it simple! Here, I'm applying duct tape to show this rider exactly where to place her hands for a One-Rein Stop.**

why they like me, it's not because I'm doing anything terribly different or much better than anybody else. It's because I can make it easy for people to understand—I keep it simple (photo 1.2)!

All clinicians are really telling the same story. Sure, we might have different ways of getting there, but we're all giving the same basic message: get the horse respectful—you want respect without fear—and get the horse soft, supple, relaxed, and collected. Just like there are a lot of different ways of getting to Chicago—from the north, south, east, or west—there's no right way or wrong way to train horses. Horses don't learn perfectly and neither do human beings. What this lesson taught me was that the simpler you keep it, the easier it is to understand—and the easier it is for the human to understand, the easier it is to get the horse to understand.

I'll be the first to tell you that I'm not the sharpest pencil in the box. But I realized that day that if I was ever going to understand horse training and horsemanship, I was going to have to take this complicated kind of instruction and make it simpler and easier to understand. In fact, I needed it to be completely idiot-proof. That's why I laugh today when I tell people that the definition of The Clinton Anderson Method is actually what I call "idiot-proof horsemanship." Not because the people I teach are idiots, but because I felt like an idiot trying to figure it all out.

Keeping it simple

So once I realized this great truth about horsemanship, anytime instructors told me what to do, I'd listen, rearrange it in my mind, and repeat it back to them—but in a much more simplified version. Then they'd either say, "Yes, Clinton, that is right." or "No, Clinton, that is wrong." If it was wrong, I'd have another go at it until I got it right. Still to this day, when I hear something new about horsemanship, I listen to it, rearrange it, and then give my version—and, what I say is *always* much more simple.

I'm not naturally talented at training horses. There are a lot of other men and women who are more gifted than I am. What I am naturally gifted and talented at is getting people to understand what I want them to do. What I discovered is that when something is easy for people to understand, it also usually works out to be easy for the horse to understand, as well. Likewise, if it's difficult for you to understand, it's going to be difficult for your horse to understand—and then neither of you makes any progress. Let's face it. If you don't get it, your horse isn't going to get it, and then no one is going to get it. It's just that simple.

I've also learned over the years that when you break horse training into small steps that are easy and simple to understand, you'll move along very quickly. Horses are very smart, but they can't connect too many dots all together at once. If you can take them from A to B, then from B to C, and then C to D, you can eventually get them to go from A to D all in one step. But if you start out trying to teach A, B, C, and D all in the same lesson, all at the same time, you're going to have trouble and confuse your horse (photos 1.3 A–C).

Exaggerate to teach and refine as you go along

Look at training horses very much the same way you would teach young children. At first, you exaggerate each step to teach it, and then, as the horse understands, you can refine your cues to be much more subtle. What do you do when you first begin to teach a child the alphabet? You exaggerate the way you sound out all the letters. Then, once he starts to recognize the letters, you don't have to say them in such an exaggerated way. Pretty soon, you don't even have to sound the letters at all. When you're teaching a small child how to write his name, are you concerned with how neat his handwriting is? Of course not! All you're concerned about at first is that he gets the right letters in the right order. As he develops his skills, his handwriting naturally gets more legible (unless he eventually turns into a doctor or lawyer and then you won't be able to read it at all).

The point is, you don't get critical about how they perform a task at first. You don't expect a lot when they're learning, because they're learning. I call the first time you try to teach your horse something new the "concept lesson." Once a horse understands the basic concept of what you want him to do, you can slowly start to work on perfection from that day forward.

The more knowledge you have, the more powerful and confident you become

Most of the time when people get frustrated with themselves and their horses, it is because they have "run out of knowledge." That's why I always say, "Frustration begins where knowledge ends." As a kid, I can remem-

1.3 A–C **Horses are very smart, but they cannot connect all the dots and go from A to D all at once. That's why we work in steps: A to B, B to C, and then C to D. Here I am helping this young woman teach her horse to flex his head and neck. Although this is ultimately one motion, the horse must learn it in stages:**

A to B: she slides her hand down the lead rope, picks up on the rope toward the horse's withers, and holds that pressure until the horse gives to it bending his head around, even slightly. She rewards the horse by immediately releasing the pressure and putting slack in the lead rope.

B to C: Now she continues to ask for a little more give each time until the horse learns to touch his nose to his side every time she slides her hand down and picks up lightly on the lead rope.

C to D: Once her horse is flexing to pressure on the halter from the same side, she refines this exercise even more. Now she begins the same process, but this time standing behind the horse's opposite shoulder, teaching her horse to give and flex to the slightest pressure on the halter.

ber being in the round pen with my horse, crying and losing my temper because I wanted my horse to do a particular exercise and I couldn't figure out how to get him to do it. I had run out of knowledge.

So what did I do? I got more knowledge. The way to get more knowledge and experience is to read more books, watch more DVDs, go to more clinics, seminars, and tours—and train more horses. Make it your passion—as it was mine—to continuously learn more about interacting with horses, what "makes them tick," and better ways to communicate with them.

I'm the prime example of somebody not naturally gifted at training horses who, because of a passion for knowledge and a deep understanding of the importance of keeping things simple, is able to achieve extraordinary results (photo 1.4). It's out there for you, too, and it's just that simple. All you have to do is go get it. The more knowledge you get, and the more you can keep it simple, the better results you'll achieve with your horses.

You only live once, mate, so go out there and get it!

1.4 **The more knowledge you have, the further your horsemanship can go. When you follow my Method, you'll see how its exercises build upon one another to increase knowledge and understanding step by step for both you and your horse. Before you know it, you will be teaching your horse advanced tricks such as sitting, as my horse, Diez, is doing here, and liberty maneuvers you never dreamed possible!**

Lesson 2

Desensitizing and sensitizing is a matter of balance

Tailoring your mix of sensitizing and desensitizing exercises will bring about the best of both worlds in every horse.

I LIFTED *the saddle pad to throw it on my horse's back.*

Wild-eyed, he sat back, snapped the lead rope, and destroyed yet another halter. It was the third time that week it had happened— not to mention how he had now started to run sideways every time I went to put my foot in the stirrup to get on, or how he spun around and bolted whenever someone tried to hand me something from the ground. What had happened to this horse?

I was 13 years old, and just two weeks had passed since Gordon McKinlay's horsemanship clinic—my first clinic, and my first experience with what I would later come to understand is a delicate balance between doing sensitizing and desensitizing exercises with a horse. Before Gordon's clinic this horse had been a bombproof backyard pet!

I called Gordon and said, "Listen, I'm getting some really good results with my horses in some areas, but they're getting very jumpy and very spooky in others."

"Have you been doing any of the desensitizing exercises?" Gordon asked.

"Well no, I haven't really been doing any of those."

"Well, you might want to go back and do more."

Now Gordon didn't say how many to do or how long to do them, he just said, "go back and do more." So, being the structured sort of person I am, I went back to the list I had made of the exercises Gordon had taught at his clinic, and after each of the ground-

Left: 2.1 **If you don't balance the fun-to-do sensitizing exercises with enough desensitizing exercises, your horse may become reactive to even ordinary things—like this horse. He has become so sensitive that even trying to put a saddle blanket on him causes him to spook and pull back.**

work and riding exercises, I wrote, "Desensitize." After about three days of following this revised list, I was absolutely amazed at the result. All of the cool new things my horses were learning, such as moving off my leg pressure, collecting, and sliding to a stop, actually got a lot better. But more importantly, all of the spooky, jumpy, reactive behavior just completely disappeared. My horses went back to being safe and quiet—but also became even more agile and responsive to my requests to move their feet.

This lesson taught me how to achieve the best of both worlds—first, a horse that would say, "Yes, Sir!" and move whenever I asked him, and second, relax and practically fall asleep anytime I didn't want his feet to move. I never made the mistake of skipping desensitizing exercises again!

The clinic I had attended with Gordon McKinlay at his place in Longreach, Queensland, was my first true experience at a horsemanship clinic. Up to that point, I had taken a lot of riding lessons and tried to read books and watch videos, but I had never been to anything "hands-on." When the clinic finished, I knew one thing for sure: I really wanted to make my living training horses. Until then, I hadn't realized that you could get paid to be around a horse. Once I realized this, it was all over! All I wanted to do was train horses.

Gordon McKinlay and Ian Francis (a champion cutter and reiner in Australia—see p. 4) taught me about 80 percent of what I now know. The other 20 percent comes from a variety of people all over the world, but the basic core fundamentals come from Gordon and Ian. And to this day, I still use the tools Gordon taught me in that clinic. Twenty years later, I'm still teaching the *same* core fundamentals.

Gordon taught us about 10 exercises to do on the ground to gain our horse's respect and about 10 riding exercises. He also showed us a few simple exercises to desensitize the horse, but he didn't really make a big deal about desensitizing. Although he did explain it and its purpose, he didn't go into much detail about it. But he did say to make sure that you do it (photos 2.2 A–C).

Two sides of the same coin

Well, when I got home from Gordon's, I only wanted to work on the *sensitizing* exercises that teach the horse to move *away* from pressure—

2.2 A–C Desensitizing the horse does not cause him to lose any of his responsiveness—it just makes him calmer, quieter, and less likely to spook and react to movement around him. Here I'm desensitizing my horse, first with the lead rope—tossing it up over and around all parts of his body.

Next, I desensitize him with my Handy Stick and String, always starting softly over his back, tossing and then dragging the string all over his body including his legs.

Then I begin the same process again, this time with a plastic bag on the end of my Handy Stick. First, I desensitize by tapping the air around the horse's body. Next, I rub him all over with the bag. Finally, I tap him all over with the bag. It is important with all of these exercises to use my Approach and Retreat Method. Approach: apply the pressure with rhythm and keep it constant until the horse stands still and relaxes; then Retreat: remove the pressure and rub the horse to reward him.

2.3.A–D **The balance ratio you need between sensitizing and desensitizing depends on a horse's temperament, but all horses need exercises doing both. Here I am doing some sensitizing groundwork with my horse.**

Disengaging the Hindquarters: I'm asking him to perform the exercise Yielding the Hindquarters—Stage One by putting pressure on his hindquarters with my body language and tapping the air with the Handy Stick. He needs to keep his inside front foot planted and cross his inside back foot in front of his outside back foot as he goes around in a 360-degree circle.

Backing: I am demonstrating Marching, one of my Method's four Backing exercises. As I march toward him with exaggerated arm movement, his job is to match my speed and stay out of my space. Backing is one of the most important groundwork exercises you can do. I back my horses everywhere!

the ones that I thought were cool like the spins, the rollbacks, the sliding stops, the sidepassing, and collection. I thought all those boring exercises like *Desensitizing to the Rope*, and to the *Handy Stick and String* that involved getting your horse to stand still, relax, or *not move to* pressure, were just for beginners. I thought they were for people who had all day and nothing better to do. How was that silly stuff really going to help me in a polocrosse match?

At that time, polocrosse—a fast-paced Australian sport that combines the most exciting elements of polo and lacrosse—was what was uppermost in my mind. To win at polocrosse, you needed to have a horse that would stop, spin, rollback, sidepass, and be very agile on his feet. Gordon's sensitizing exercises made my horses so responsive I couldn't believe it (photos 2.3 A–D)!

When I left that clinic so impressed with what I had learned, I was worried that I might forget everything. So, on the way home, I wrote down all the exercises on an old envelope I found in the back seat of the car. Every time I went to the barn, I'd take that envelope with me and go through the exercises. Number One: Yield the Hindquarters; Number Two: Back Up; Number Three: Yield the Forequarters, and so on. (See my book, *Clinton Anderson's Downunder Horsemanship* for a list and detailed

Lungeing: Here I am sending my horse off with energy in my Lungeing for Respect exercise. Notice how he is quiet and attentive. There is slack in the lead line but energy in his feet as he moves around me in a nice, even circle.

Sending: This exercise is good for sensitizing your horse to pressure from the halter on his poll—and at the same time it works as a desensitizing exercise that teaches him to go calmly through narrow spaces and move past spooky objects.

information about these essential exercises on the ground and under saddle.) I'd just run through the whole list of all these exercises every day.

After about two weeks, I was absolutely amazed at the results. My horses were becoming a lot more soft and supple, and were actually starting to do all the great things I had seen horses do in fancy American horse magazines, like slide to a stop, back up, collect, spin, and rollback. However, they also started to become very reactive: this spookiness and jumpiness didn't happen over night, but progressively got worse. After two more weeks of this, the horses became downright dangerous.

As a result of that call to Gordon I began to understand the concept of sensitizing versus desensitizing. What I learned in this lesson is that when we want a horse to move in response to our pressure, that's *sensitizing;* when we want the horse to stand still and ignore pressure, that's *desensitizing.* Pressure, for a horse, comes from outside stimulus in the form of sight, sound, or touch. When we're sensitizing a horse, we're asking him to pay attention to whatever stimulus we're using to cue him. When we're desensitizing a horse, what we're actually doing is teaching him to ignore a stimulus.

When Gordon gave me his advice to go back and desensitize, I learned a valuable lesson that has stayed with me ever since. When you

2.4 **I want a horse that is responsive when I want him to move, but when I ask him to stand still and fall asleep, he'll do so in a heartbeat. My horse, Mindy, loves it when I relax my body language, because she knows that is her opportunity for a well-earned rest.**

sensitize a horse too much, you may well get him respectful and moving his feet whenever you want him to, but he may also become quite reactive and difficult. If you desensitize a horse too much, he may well become quiet and relaxed, but he won't want to move, and may become resentful, pushy, and disrespectful. However, when you create good balance between your sensitizing and desensitizing, what you get is the best of both worlds: a horse that will say "Yes, sir!" when you tell him to move, and fall asleep when you tell him to relax (photo 2.4).

Get creative

If you're having trouble thinking of ways to desensitize your horse, just get two or three kids together and ask them what they'd do (photos 2.5 A & B). Children have some of the most creative minds in the world, and if you watch them with horses, they're often climbing and flopping around all over them. That's why kids tend to do a great job of desensitizing; however, because they are less structured, not as disciplined or consistent as adults, they do a poor job of sensitizing. Adults, on the other hand, because they tend to be more cautious and less imaginative, often are much poorer at desensitizing.

Adjusting to fit

Now of course, some horses require more of one category than the other. For example, if you have a very hot, nervous, reactive type of horse, you might have to spend more time desensitizing him to pressure. If you've got a cold-blooded, lazy horse, you might spend more time sensitizing him to pressure.

It is important to understand that there are hot-blooded horses and there are cold-blooded horses. Hot-blooded horses are very smart, athletic, and sensitive. They like to go, go, go. These generally include Arabs, Thoroughbreds, and some bloodlines of Quarter Horses. Cold-blooded horses, on the other hand, are more laid back and good-natured. These are often draft horses, Friesians, and some bloodlines of gaited horses and Quarter Horses. As a general rule, they are reluctant to move and usually don't learn as quickly, either. It just takes them longer to catch on. You're always telling these horses, "Come on! Hurry up, let's move!"

To find the right balance between sensitizing and desensitizing your horse, you'll need to consider your horse's breeding, bloodlines, and personality. You can't just say that all Quarter Horses are hot or that all draft breeds are cold. Bloodlines within a breed can go either way. Some Quarter Horse bloodlines produce very hot, athletic, and sensitive animals, while others are fat, lazy, and "fall over their own shadow." To simply say that a certain breed or type of horse is always athletic or always cold-blooded just isn't true.

2.5 A & B **Get creative, and if you're looking for ideas, ask some kids to assist you! Kids are the greatest "desensitizers" in the world. I invited these two kids to bring their noisiest toys, their loudest voices, and their silliest moves to try and scare Jillaroo. When Jillaroo relaxed and lowerd her head, I asked my young friend to retreat and rub her.**

A new day, every day

Remember that the weather greatly affects how your horse feels. When the weatherman says that it's a cold, rainy, and windy day, he might as well say that if you own a horse and are going to ride, get ready to die! These natural elements make horses hypersensitive. On cold days, they like to gallop around the pasture and kick up their heels. On windy days they hear, smell, and see things move all over the place. Their senses are on overload, and they are constantly reacting. What are horses like in the middle of summer when it's really hot? Most of them are really quiet, laid back, and lethargic.

Remember to take these factors into consideration when you are planning your mix of sensitizing and desensitizing exercises to fit not only your horse's breeding and personality, but also any changes in circumstances that could affect his behavior. Your horse's temperament, the weather conditions, how much you're feeding him and how much turnout he has all must go into determining how frisky he will be when you work with him. You must stay aware and constantly balance sensitizing and desensitizing with the situation at hand if you are to avoid the mistake I made by focusing on one to the exclusion of the other.

Lesson 3

Do what you have to do to get the job done

Building better communication with your horse really comes about by making the right things easy and the wrong things difficult — and always rewarding the slightest try.

THE big black mare eyed me from the other side of the pen. Her nostrils flared, her tail swished, and it was obvious that the very last thing she wanted was for me to catch her and get to work.

I was about 15 or 16 years old, training horses in Australia for Gordon McKinlay, and I was just getting started with the whole natural horsemanship thing. Following my early training, as soon as that mare would do something right, I would instantly reward her. I would pat her, give her a little treat, and let her rest to encourage good behavior and a good attitude. I was basically trying to bribe her into loving me and loving what she was doing by constantly rewarding her. And ironically, she was actually getting worse every day.

Gordon took one look at this belligerent mare and said, "Clinton, this mare is not looking very good at all. You've done a pretty bad job on this horse." Gordon has never been one to mince words.

I said, "Gordon, I've been working with this horse seven days a week, doing everything you taught me, trying my best to get her where she needs to be—but she's just got a bad attitude."

"Well, you'd better just step up to the plate and get the job done," he said, "because this mare has to go home next week and the owners are not going to be very happy with you—or with me—if they come and see how bad she is after being here for six weeks."

So, here's what I did:

For the entire last week of her training, I treated that mare like I would any other regular horse. I got in there every day and *made the wrong thing difficult and the right thing easy. If she didn't move, I made her feet move—NOW. I asked her, told her, asked her, told her, asked her, told her. I didn't care about her feelings. I didn't care about her emotions. I didn't care about her attitude. When she did something right, I let her rest and I left her alone. When she did something wrong, I made her feel very uncomfortable.*

Within three days, that mare's attitude—and her whole perception of work, and of me—completely changed. In fact, in that last week of working with her, I caught her up to where she should have been by that time, despite our initial setbacks. On the day she went home, she was as good as all the other horses that had been ridden for six weeks. She made more progress in those last five or six days than she had in the entire five weeks before.

This cranky black mare taught me a lesson in natural horsemanship I will never forget. Gordon was teaching me the techniques he knew, and I was eagerly absorbing every detail. I was also reading everything I could get my hands on about natural horsemanship, and I was really into achieving this whole "I love you, you love me, we're going to bond together" kind of experience with every horse I trained. In his book, *True Unity*, Tom Dorrance had written about how everything should just come together, flow together, and how easy it all should be. But as this horse pointed out, something was missing in my understanding of how to really put natural horsemanship into practice.

The problem with this mare was that she had a really bad attitude. She was sour, she was grumpy, and she never wanted to do anything. She was just a belligerent type with no work ethic whatsoever—and a heart the size of a pea. Nevertheless, I was determined to teach her to love me, to love her job, and to have a better attitude. I had been working with this mare for nearly five of the six weeks we used to break in all our horses, and she was way behind schedule. To look at her and how she behaved, you would think she was only in her second or third week of training.

Don't get emotional

I think sometimes people get so worried about their relationship with their horse and so wrapped up in this whole natural horsemanship thing that they forget the bottom line: you've got to get the job done. The rea-

3.2 **If a horse doesn't like what you ask him to do, as this one is telling Krista with his pinned-back ears, turn up the heat! Here Krista is doing just that with lots of changes of direction, making the horse work even harder, telling him, "If you don't like this, try THIS!"**

son why that mare's attitude never got any better was because I was "babysitting" her. I was trying to coax her into liking me. I was trying to persuade her to like the situation.

What she really needed from me was a taste of long rides, "wet saddle blankets," and concentrated training (we'll get more into that in Lesson 4). She needed a taste of, "If you don't like this, try this. If you thought what I was asking you to do was difficult and sweaty, how about this." After I did that for a few days, her attitude came around like you wouldn't believe. She realized that if she didn't want to do what I asked, I was just going to make everything a lot harder than she really wanted it. And in turn, she realized that what I was originally asking her to do was not so bad after all (photo 3.2)!

Thanks to that mare, I learned a very important aspect of natural horsemanship that a lot of people don't understand. Although I certainly do want my horses to like me and to enjoy the time we spend together (don't get me wrong—that's still very important to me), the reality is this: when you're training a horse, you have a job to do, and you've got to get that job done (photo 3.3).

Horses are a lot like people—their personalities vary—and some horses, like some people, are just naturally cranky. Can you improve their attitude? Sure you can. But you may never get them to put a smile on their face all the time. Some horses, on the other hand, you can never offend. You can never make them mad. You can never insult them. With some people, you can just look at them sideways and they get angry and hateful. And yet with others, you can insult their mother and they just smile at you and say, "Oh you don't really mean that. Come over here and let me give you a hug."

There are also some horses—just like some people—that are just sorry-bred or sorry-minded. Not every person that goes to jail is going to be rehabilitated, and not every belligerent horse is going to change his attitude, no matter what you do. It's just that simple.

The lesson I learned from that difficult black mare is one I hope people will relate to—on many levels. I have a lot of people in my program that are so hooked on this whole lovey-dovey "I love my horse, she loves me" emotion that they miss the fact they're basically begging their horse to do what they want him to do.

When you focus too much on those emotions and lose sight of the bottom line—getting the job done—you get the opposite of what you're looking for. Before you can have that emotional connection and relationship with your horse, you first have to earn his respect by getting the job done of moving his feet—forward, backward, left, and right.

I've remembered this lesson ever since the day I watched that mare loaded onto the trailer to go home. I still want my horses to enjoy their jobs. I still want to reward the slightest try. However, the bottom line is, I am going to get the job done. If the horse doesn't like it, tough luck—I'm going to do it anyway.

I've discovered by applying this lesson over the years that for horses with the worst attitudes, the less you ask them to do and the less pressure you put on them, the worse they get. And conversely, the harder you work them and the more you ask them to do, the better their attitudes get. Although you may never turn a fundamentally sour-minded horse into the horse of your dreams, by always focusing first on getting the job done, you're always going to get the best possible results with that particular horse.

3.3 Instead of begging for a sour-minded horse's cooperation, just do what you have to do to get the job done. Here I'm doing a series of Rollbacks on the Fence, a great way to improve his attitude by moving his feet.

Lesson 4

Long rides, "wet saddle pads," and concentrated training

Structuring your training time in these three equal parts will give you the key to achieving a quiet, dependable, yet supple and responsive horse.

EVERY

time I circle the arena during a tour to demonstrate Mindy's slow, easy, collected lope, I always hear the whispers. Everyone wants to know how I taught Mindy to lope so slowly. In fact, with everything Mindy does, she tries to conserve her energy. Why? Because I've put lots of miles under her feet. If I start riding Mindy at 7:00 A.M., she has no idea if I'm going to get off her at 7:15 A.M. or if I'm going to get off at 7:15 P.M.—she always places her bet that it's going to be P.M.

When I put a beginner on Mindy, within about two minutes she's figured out that the rider doesn't know a lot, and she just walks real slow, jogs real slow, and doesn't overreact to anything he does. Then I can get on Mindy and within two seconds she's doing a flying lead change every other stride. That's what good horses do. Good horses don't take advantage of a rider who doesn't know very much; good horses adapt to the rider's ability. To me, a truly great horse is one that I can take into competition and do well, and then take out on the trail without him being spooky, jumpy, or reactive.

Mindy's a good horse. There's no doubt about that. But what makes her such a good horse? Sure she's bred well, trained well, and has a wonderful temperament. But there's a secret formula Gordon taught me years ago that is the absolute key to training. In her life, Mindy has had a steady dose of this formula—and the result speaks for itself.

Left: 4.1 **The perfect formula for getting a well-broke horse is an equal mixture of long rides, "wet saddle blankets," and concentrated training. Consistent use of this formula yields amazing results.**

"Clinton," Gordon used to say, "to get a truly broke horse takes three things: long rides, wet saddle blankets, and concentrated training—and you have to have equal doses of all three."

Is this lesson really a secret? Of course not! The key to it that lots of people miss, however, is that you must have *all* of these things, balanced in *three equal parts*. Lots of ranch horses get *long rides*—they're ridden all day from sunup to sundown, but they're stiff as a board in their face and body. Plenty of show horses are soft and supple from all the concentrated training they get, but try taking one out on the trail and he'll probably half kill you as he reacts to and spooks at everything he sees—scary objects, water, dogs, whatever. And, racehorses almost always come back with wet saddle blankets, but try to do something with them besides gallop and you'll see what's missing in their training.

As soon as you have one third that's bigger than the other two thirds, the formula just doesn't work as well. However, if you consistently give your horse three equal doses of long rides, "wet saddle blankets," and concentrated training, you'll have a truly great, soft, supple, respectful, and collected horse that you can ride in the arena, show, and compete, as well as ride out on the trail, use to gather up cattle, and know is a safe, dependable partner.

Long rides

What exactly do I mean by "long rides"? What many people don't realize is that a long ride without a wet saddle pad is completely useless. If you go on a five-hour trail ride, walk the entire time, and when you get back and take the saddle off there isn't one ounce of sweat on your horse's body, you've accomplished very little in terms of training.

So one thing "long rides" does mean is that you've got to put some miles under your horse's feet *at all three gaits*—walk, trot, and canter. The best way to do this is to take your horse out on a big dirt road. In Australia, I trained a lot of my horses on dirt roads. Trot him for three to four miles, and then lope him for three to four miles—just put some steady miles under his feet. You'll be amazed how much more a horse remembers when you travel some distance and he gets a little tired (photo 4.2). Usually, the quieter the horse, the more hours someone has spent in the saddle.

Keep in mind, a tired horse is a good horse. I've seen fresh horses, frisky horses, and energetic horses give people lots of problems, but I've never seen a tired horse give anyone any trouble. Now, don't take this out of context. I'm not saying "long rides" are about *exhausting* your horse in order to make him behave. It's about putting enough miles under his feet so you give him a reason to want to go slowly.

"Long rides" mean that you can't expect your horse to get broke if you just ride him for 10 minutes every day. Once a week, or at least once every other week, you've got to take him out and—if you can—go on a trail ride that lasts two to four hours.

4.2 **Long rides: There's nothing better than a long dirt road for putting miles under your horse's feet. I'm giving my horse a change of scenery as well as a long ride.**

"Wet saddle blankets"

What does "wet saddle blankets" really mean? Contrary to what some people may think, this part of the formula is not just about sweat. You can bring your horse back tired and sweaty every single day, but if all you've done is just gallop flat-out around the pasture—even when he comes back dripping with sweat—you haven't taught him anything through sweat alone.

When you ride, be sure to spend time at all three gaits and move his feet. Give him a reason to get sweaty. Try to pick a place, like a dirt track or field that gives you plenty of room: the wider the area, the more opportunities you have to train. I have a nice covered arena, but I only ride in it when the weather is bad. If it's good day, I love to ride my horses out in the paddock, on dirt roads, or wherever there's lots of room to move their feet.

To accomplish the "wet saddle blankets" part of the formula, do lots of transitions. Trot down the road, then stop and sidepass him to one side, and lope him off again. Then back up and trot down the road doing the *Serpentine* exercise. Supple all of those five body parts as you're riding down the road (photo 4.3).

To do this, string together deliberate exercises that isolate and move your horse's head and neck, poll, shoulders, rib cage, and hips. Do bending transitions to soften his head and neck. Ask for vertical flexion at the walk, trot, and canter to supple his poll. Practice the *Shoulder-In, Shoulder-Out* exercise to move his shoulders. Then do some *Two-Tracking* to move his rib cage. *Yield to a Stop* transitions will supple his hips. You can find all of these exercises in my *Riding with Confidence* DVD series. If every time you ride your horse you

4.3 **"Wet saddle blankets": Do lots of transitions wherever you go, both inside and outside the arena. You can see I'm bending my horse in a circle; next, I'll sidepass him a few steps; then we'll lope off. Mixing things up makes it interesting for the horse and keeps the "thinking" side of his brain engaged.**

make sure to "oil all these hinges" and move his feet forward, back, left, and right until you get that saddle blanket wet, you'll be amazed at how quiet, soft, and supple he'll become.

Concentrated training

What is "concentrated training?" It's basically what I teach people in clinics: getting your horse soft, supple, and relaxed; getting him moving off your leg pressure; and getting your horse to collect. That's what you teach your horse in the arena. However, "concentrated training" in Gordon's secret formula means much more than just training your horse in the arena and always bringing him back with a wet saddle pad. A lot of show horses are trained so much in the arena that they come to resent

4.4 **Concentrated training: This is anything that gives your horse a sense of purpose. Giving a horse a job he likes to do makes learning more fun for both of you! My cow horse prospect, Barron, practices chasing a cow down the fence. Working cattle is great for a horse's mind because cows are unpredictable and no two days are ever the same.**

their job. They're the ones you see swishing their tails, pinning their ears and getting cranky because they never have any sense of purpose to what they're doing (photo 4.4).

One of the things I used to love was when Gordon and I would go out mustering cattle all day, and the whole time we would be training our horses. We'd bend and supple as we moved along. If we were walking behind the cattle, we'd sidepass for a while, then walk on a loose rein for five minutes, and then we'd bend and do serpentines. We would train our horses like that for eight hours straight, and they would never get sour or irritated because it was fun for them to have a purpose. We were just doing our training exercises as we gathered and moved the cattle.

Whenever you give a horse a purpose, he enjoys his life much more. When a horse doesn't have that sense of purpose, occasionally he will get bored eventually and start to resent his job. However, while variety and purpose are important, finding the right balance is crucial. If you have too much variety without consistency, the horse never learns anything; too much consistency without variety, and the horse gets bored.

So do your three equal doses while you're out on the trail: take your horse on long rides, bring him back with a wet saddle pad, and give him concentrated training along the way. Then you, too, will end up with a truly great horse.

Lesson 5

Heart attacks are free

The more you try to scare a horse when you're desensitizing the less reactive he'll become — and the more you "sneak around" the spookier he'll get.

THE
horse galloped sideways away from me and I had his head tipped toward me at a 90-degree angle to avoid his heels. As I was dragged through the air, my feet hitting the ground every 15 to 20 feet, I yelled at this horse and slapped the stirrup against the saddle and ran at him as fast as I could.

Even though this had been going on for about three minutes, it felt like three hours. Since my number one rule is never to lose my temper when I'm training a horse, I was clearly having an out-of-body temper explosion.

This three-year-old gelding was the most reactive horse I had ever encountered. I was leading him to the arena and he had shied—probably at his own shadow—and jumped over the top of me, stepping on the back of my spur, and knocking me all the way to the ground. I had been working with this horse for four weeks, and he was still spooky and jumpy. Every time I went to touch him or move around him he would always react and get defensive.

Now I'm not proud of my reaction. But, even as furious as I was, I was not physically hurting this horse—I was simply trying to "kill him with fear." After we were both completely exhausted, he stopped. I didn't stop him—he just stopped. Doubled over, gasping for breath, I still kept slapping the stirrup, but he just stood there. I was about to pass out and just lay down on the ground. His nostrils were flaring about 20 miles an hour and we were both drenched in sweat and completely out of air.

After about 10 minutes, I got my weary body upright and we

Left: 5.1 **A horse that is spooky and jumpy under saddle is no fun to ride. This horse is reacting to me flapping the stirrup. All this tells me is that he needs me to keep flapping and following him until he discovers that it's not going to hurt him, stands still, and relaxes. Then and only then will I stop the flapping and reward him.**

eyed each other. I approached the horse, fully expecting to have to start all over again with him. I thought for sure the horse would be absolutely scared to death of me, and I'd just wrecked the last four weeks of really hard work. I wasn't upset with the horse, but I was upset with myself for losing my temper.

To my surprise, when I reached up to rub the horse on the neck, he did not react at all. His head stayed down low to the ground, and even when I slapped the stirrup a little bit, he didn't move a muscle. I tightened the girth and got straight on him, and he was as quiet as a kid's pony. At the end of the ride, I took the saddle off and threw it back on him—no reaction whatsoever. From that point on, this horse, aptly named Shakin' All Over, was absolutely bombproof, teaching me a lesson I'll never forget about desensitization.

What I learned from Shakin' All Over is that with some horses you have to be more extreme to get your point across. If you want to be effective, you have to be understood. Whenever I have a horse that's overly reactive all the time every single day, that tells me that I'm not being "scary" enough. I'm not pushing him through that resistance.

With a horse like this, you may have to become a lot "scarier" than you normally want to be. For example, when I raise my hand up toward a horse's eye to rub him and he throws his head up, I then flap my hand up and down right beside his eye and try to "kill him" with his own fear of my hand (photo 5.2).

Of course, I'm not going to hurt him—such an approach would never work. You just want the horse to *think* you could, without ever actually hitting him. If I had hit that horse as he was running sideways away from me, it would have just proved to him that there was a reason to be frightened of me.

To me, the worst possible thing that can happen when desensitizing a horse (other than me getting killed or the horse getting hurt) is for the horse to actually get away from me. That reinforces both the horse's fear and his idea that running to escape is the right answer. What I did with that horse in the story above worked because I stayed with him for several minutes, continuing to apply the same pressure no matter what he did. The reason it worked was because the only time I took away the pressure—meaning the only time I stopped flapping the stirrup—was when he stood still and had completely relaxed.

From that point on, I started getting really good results with that horse. With him, I realized that what I had been doing wrong was tak-

5.2 **With some horses, you have to be as "scary" as possible to get your point across. Maybe it's ironic, but the more you try to scare your horse, the calmer he will become.**

ing the pressure away *too soon*. When you're desensitizing a horse, quitting too early will always cause problems. You won't have a problem if you desensitize for too long, but you can definitely cause difficulties by stopping too soon.

Two ways to desensitize: "progressive desensitization" vs. "flooding"

There are two different ways to desensitize a horse to objects that spook him. These are what we call "progressive desensitization" and "flooding"—a technique generally reserved for foals.

Progressive desensitization is exactly that—you progressively move a "scary" object or noise toward the horse to eventually get him used to it.

5.3 A **"Progressive desensitization" means using my Approach and Retreat technique to gradually increase a horse's tolerance to a particular "scary" object or sound. I'm flapping the plastic bag all around my horse until he stands still and relaxes. When he does relax, I'll stop flapping, retreat, and rub him.**

Begin far enough away from the horse so you can establish a starting point. Remember that the closer the item is, the more he will probably react. Slowly use the method called *Approach and Retreat*. You *approach* the horse and then, when his feet stand still and he shows you a sign he's relaxing, *retreat* by taking the object away. Bring the item that frightens him a little closer each time—then retreat—until eventually you can touch the horse with the object and move it all around his body (photos 5.3 A & B).

With flooding your goal is to "flood" all of the horse's senses—sight, smell, hearing, and touch. Flooding these four senses teaches the horse to accept that whatever he is normally scared of is not going to hurt him. It basically forces the horse to accept the object, noise, or sensation. You are either confining him somehow (as you can with foals), or chasing him as I did with Shakin' All Over. The point is to keep the pressure on—the same kind at the same intensity—until the horse physically and mentally just gives up and becomes submissive. And when he becomes submissive, he doesn't get hurt, he doesn't get in trouble, he can completely relax.

Now, as a general rule, you only want to flood foals. Robert M. Miller, DVM, who is considered the father of the revolutionary foal training technique known as "imprint training," has developed a fantastic method for getting a horse to accept desensitizing. Dr. Miller's imprinting procedure begins when a foal is born and still lying on the ground—before he even

5.3 B **Eventually, progressive desensitization allows you to bring the object a little closer until you can put it anywhere on the horse's body without getting a reaction. Here my horse is accepting the bag and letting me rub it all over his face. This is the result of progressive desensitization with this plastic bag over several sessions.**

gets up. You begin by touching the foal all over; you rub plastic bags all over his body; get him used to the clippers; and you put your finger in his nose, around his gums, and in his ears. You tap the bottoms of his feet. You rub him down with paper bags so they make a noise.

Through all this, you keep the foal down on the ground. Anytime he struggles and tries to escape by getting up, you physically force him back to the ground until he relaxes. When he submits to the object being placed on him, you take it away for a moment, and then you do it again. By taking away the foal's natural flight response, he learns to be submissive.

There are three ways to control a horse's mind—you can create movement, redirect movement, and inhibit movement (i.e., hobble, or lay the horse down and take away his legs as you do when imprinting foals). Once a horse gets much bigger than a foal, of course he gets much stronger, and as an adult horse, he is very strong. Flooding then becomes less of an option.

Although *Approach and Retreat* is always used as a first option for older horses, in extreme cases flooding, done correctly, can be used effectively by an experienced horse trainer to achieve desired results. The key word, however, is "correctly." If done *incorrectly*, flooding can be absolutely disastrous. The horse can get hurt, the human can get hurt, and the horse can learn to be even more fearful than he was before you started the lesson.

The first foal that I imprinted, I completely ruined. I was about 14, I'd read Dr. Robert Miller's book, and I tried to imprint this foal. I was in a hurry, though, and I had to feed the other horses. So I stayed with the foal for about 20 minutes and rubbed him up and down and tapped his legs, and so on. Just before I left, he was starting to struggle and get up. I knew I needed to keep going with him longer—I knew I wasn't done yet—but I decided to go feed some horses, do some chores, and then come back and finish.

When I came back two hours later, that foal was the wildest thing God had ever put on the earth. I couldn't even get near him; he was so crazy. When I eventually got my hands on him, he was rearing up and jumping and trying to run through my arms. Even at only a few hours old, he acted like a wild Mustang. I said to myself, "I thought this imprinting stuff was supposed to make this horse quieter and gentler!"

Well, when I went back and studied Dr. Miller's book again, I realized what I had done wrong. I quit when the horse was trying to get up. If I had stayed with the foal and held him on the ground and waited until he became relaxed and submissive before I walked away, he would have become quieter. But I actually taught the foal to be wild because I took the pressure away as he was kicking, striking, and trying to get up.

Although most clinicians really promote progressive desensitization for adult horses rather than flooding, there are some situations where flooding can work very well. What I didn't realize at the time was that I was actually desensitizing Shakin' All Over using the flooding technique.

There are a couple problems with trying to flood an older horse. You've heard the saying, "The bigger they are, the harder they fall." Well, the same thing with a horse: the bigger the horse, the harder it is to physically restrain him. And, when you *do* restrain an adult horse, it's very easy for him to get hurt as he kicks, bucks, struggles, and even flips over in panic. So, as I said, flooding becomes less of an option as a horse grows older, but still, when done correctly by a professional trainer, flooding a horse can bring tremendous results.

Keep the pressure on

My mistake with Shakin' All Over was that although I had been doing a lot of *Approach and Retreat*, I was retreating too soon—before the horse actually showed me signs of relaxing. I was taking away the pressure when there was still a little bit of tension in his muscles, his head was still a little bit high, and there was still a little bit of a wild look in his eye. Every time I retreated when there was still fear and resistance in the horse, that fear and resistance just "grew back" over night. That's why at the end of one training session, I could have him really quiet, then come back the next day to train him and have to start all over again. That little bit of resistance I left in him was actually "multiplying" and I had my spooky, crazy horse back.

What this experience taught me was that there are times you need to be a lot "scarier" than what the horse thinks you really are. I try to "kill a horse with my scariness"; that's what I mean when I often say, "Heart attacks are free." You have to keep the pressure on and wait until the horse's feet stop moving and he shows signs of relaxing—including dropping his head, licking his lips, cocking a hind leg, blinking his eyes, or taking a deep breath.

Remember, when you're desensitizing a horse, the more you try to scare him, the quieter and more relaxed he'll become. I know it doesn't sound right, but it really is true. If you always sneak around your horse and try never to startle him, what generally happens is the horse gets even more spooky and reactive.

Lesson 6

Get your horse "city-slicker broke"

Getting creative in your desensitization will train a horse for the way *anyone* might ride him — and will teach him to stay calm when the unexpected occurs.

I HAD

done a great job training this five-year-old, green-broke, ranch gelding. The horse belonged to a rich cattleman who had told me that if I did a good job, he'd bring me 15 to 20 horses a year to break in. As an 18-year-old, nearly starving horse trainer just starting out on his own, this sounded to me like the opportunity of a lifetime.

After six weeks of working with this horse for a good two hours every single day, I was really happy with his progress. He could stop, spin, sidepass, and back in circles; you could move all five body parts, ride him outside on trails, and even crack a stock whip and stand on his back. I was thinking, "Man, when this guy comes to see this horse, he's going to love me so much that he's going to give me all his horses every year."

Then came the eight words that changed everything: "Do you mind if I ride the horse?"

Now this was a very big man, maybe about 300 pounds, and the horse was probably about 15 hands. As he's grunting and groaning and pulling himself up, the horse lifted up his head and his whole body stiffened. Then he snorted, his eyes rolled back in his head, and I thought, "Uh-oh. This doesn't look good."

Then, as the man attempted to bring his right leg up over the horse, he kicked the horse squarely in the flank. That did it. The horse jumped forward, put his head down and bucked—hard. As the guy slammed into the ground head first, I thought, "This is the end of my career. If he's not dead, he's going to tell everybody

Left: 6.1 **Back in Australia when training a horse for someone, I quickly learned that for him to be happy, I had to train the horse for him to ride— and not the way I would ride him. So, for a few days before a horse went home, I did "special" desensitizing to get him ready for anything that particular owner might do. I called this getting a horse "city-slicker broke."**

in the entire world that I did a terrible job. I'm finished. My career as a trainer is over."

I ran over. "Are you okay?" I asked, helping him up off the ground and trying to brush some of the dirt off him. Not only was he covered in dirt, he also had a bloody nose, and I expected him to be really upset with me.

Luckily, this guy was easy to get along with, and he actually took the episode really well. He said, "No, Clinton, I kicked him in the flank when I went to get on. It wasn't his fault—it was my mistake."

I went and caught the horse and got right up. The horse stood there like a 10-year-old gelding. I got on and off several more times, and each time he stood perfectly still.

Then I had an idea.

I bent the gelding's head around and got halfway up in the saddle, and then I lightly kicked him on the flank. The horse jumped away and tried to buck. So I just kept doing that, over and over, until I could climb awkwardly about halfway on, kick him in the flank, and he'd stand there and completely ignore me.

I said to the guy, "Will you please leave him with me for two more weeks? I won't charge you a cent." He agreed, and when the guy came back two weeks later and climbed up on the horse exactly the same way he had the first time, even managing to kick him in the flank, the horse just stood there. The big man and his horse taught me a valuable lesson: It doesn't matter what I can do with a horse. What matters is what I can get you to do with your horse.

This lesson (learned the hard way) has stayed with me my whole career. I'll never forget the image of handing that guy the reins and watching him walk up to that horse like a great big old grizzly bear. What I learned from that lesson was that especially wild horses, or horses that haven't had a lot of handling by human beings, can get very used to how one person does something.

Up until then, I thought that the way I got on a horse was the way that everybody got on. I assumed that, like me, they'd try to help the horse out by giving a little hop, hop, hop and then swing a leg up and over and into the saddle. Unfortunately, that's not always the case. I was young and agile, so it was easy for me to do that. However, for people who are larger, older, or stiffer, it's a lot harder to get on a horse.

Before that day, I didn't realize that you have to actually train a horse for what the *owner* is going to do. I had been training every horse for a rider who was experienced and agile—not for a person who might not have very good athletic skills.

Doing it wrong to get it right

As a result of this lesson, for four days before a horse went home to his owner, I would start to "city-slicker train" him. I would spend five minutes at the end of every training session just doing silly things to him (photos 6.2 A–E). I'd slide off behind the saddle. I'd get on and off from both sides. I'd pull myself up into the saddle, and as I did it, I'd knee him in the belly and grunt. I'd "dare" the horse to run off and misbehave.

In the beginning, some horses would get worried and stick their head up in the air or move around in a circle. Occasionally, one might even try to buck a little bit. But I continued to do everything "wrong" according to proper horse etiquette, because I realized it was better to assume the worst of the owners. I'd anticipate they were going to get on the wrong way, kick the horse in the belly on their way up, or leave the reins dragging around the horse's knees.

I learned that I had to have that horse so bombproof that if you got on and spurred him in the back of the hip or dragged your spur down his back or his opposite flank, he'd just stand there. I learned how to get a horse so "city-slicker broke" that even people who didn't have enough balance to sit on a rail on a windy day couldn't spook him—no matter *what* they did.

That lesson turned out to be the foundation of what I'm doing today. I've got to help you to succeed at *your* goals, from wherever *you* happen to be. So if you need a mounting block to get on your horse, I'm going show you how to use one. If you want to get on from the right side every day and not the left side, I'm going to show you how to train your horse to accept that.

Creative desensitizing

I realized that day that the key to getting a horse to stand like a statue while his owner mounts (in whichever way he does) is to train the horse with some creative desensitizing. So, I run up to the horse "screaming" and then jump into the saddle. Or, I get on him, reach back and slap him on the rump as hard as I can to try and make him run or buck. And, the

6.2 A–D Here are some of the silly things I do to get a horse to stand still no matter what happens as the rider tries to climb aboard: I kick the horse in the rump as I swing my leg over, just as some people might accidentally do...

...drag the toe of my boot across his hip and flank...

...pretend to lose my balance and fall forward onto his neck...

...get on from right side...

...and slip out of the stirrup and fall backward, still hanging onto the horse.

last couple of minutes of every ride, I remember how tall the owner is and adjust the stirrups accordingly, or I ride the horse around and sit behind the saddle. I also get on him and lean forward and grab hold of his ears (photos 6.3 A–D).

I don't do anything that could hurt the horse, but I *dare* him to be reactive and stupid. That way, if something stupid is going to happen, it happens to me so that I can fix it.

When I get every horse I train "city-slicker broke," by the time the owner says he wants to ride the horse, I know the horse will stand like a statue. Again, what *I* can do with a horse doesn't count. What counts is what the *owner* can do with a horse.

This concept extends beyond inexperienced riders to the preferences and quirks of *any* rider. When I was breaking in colts for Ian Francis, I'd ride them for about four weeks and then he'd take over and finish them in whatever discipline he wanted. When he started complaining that none of the horses would stand still when he went to get on them, I couldn't figure out why—they stood perfectly still for me. He'd complain that every time he put his foot in the stirrup they'd start moving in a circle. He was really getting annoyed and bent out of shape about this, and I was completely baffled as to why it was happening.

6.3A–D **I also: slide off his back…**

…sit behind the saddle…

…hang on the horse's neck…

…and lean forward and grab his ears.

With each of these exercises, it is important to get your horse well desensitized with my normal desensitizing exercises first, then use Approach and Retreat to work up to these sillier and more extreme exercises.

6.4 **Desensitizing a horse's sides to the toe of a boot means he'll stand like a statue no matter how someone gets on him. Here I'm gradually putting more and more pressure on the horse's side with the toe of my boot as I get on to teach him to stand still no matter how far someone sticks their foot through the stirrup. I will also adjust the stirrup to several different heights and repeat this exercise to accommodate different heights of riders.**

Then one day I really studied what Ian was doing when he went to get on a horse. Ian is not very tall—you might say he is a bit "vertically challenged." I noticed that when he put his foot in the stirrup adjusted correctly for him, it was up a lot higher on the horse's belly than it was for me, and his foot would poke the horse's belly when he went to swing his leg over.

It wasn't hurting the horse, but it was putting pressure on him in an area where he'd never been pressured before. So every time Ian unknowingly poked a horse in the belly with the toe of his boot, the horse took it as a cue to walk forward. Actually, the horse probably thought he was doing the right thing!

Once I figured out what was going on, I changed my program a little bit. For the last three days before I gave a horse back to Ian, I'd put my stirrups up real short, and then I'd repeatedly poke the horse with the toe of my boot. I'd get the horse desensitized to that pressure so that when Ian got on, the horse would just stand there (photo 6.4).

At last, I had learned this lesson well—and even better, I had learned *how* to prepare a horse for the way he would be handled and ridden by whomever I was training him for. Using these principles, you can do exactly the same thing. Whatever you need to do, however you need to get on, and however you will be handling your horse, use your desensitizing techniques to prepare the horse and the jumpiness will disappear.

Lesson 7

Horse problems are nothing more than symptoms of a cause

Most horse problems come from either fear or lack of respect — and moving a horse's feet works to remove the underlying cause and solve the problems all at the same time.

"CLINTON

my horse is in pain." The lady standing before me at a clinic in North Carolina had spent more than $3,000 on vets, chiropractors, acupuncturists, and others to try to figure out the source of her horse's pain.

"What makes you think he's in pain?" I asked, looking at the horse.

"Every time I go to pick up his right front foot," she said, following my gaze, "he rears up in the air and strikes out like he hurts. I can pick up his other three feet absolutely perfectly, but when I try to pick up his right front foot, he rears up and leaps backward. Nobody can figure what's wrong with him: his X-rays are clean, and his chiropractor says he's fine. Do you think you can help me?"

"I think I can," I said, "but let's not address it now. Let's worry about it at the end of the clinic."

She looked confused—and a little bit miffed. "Do you promise?" she asked. "Because that's the only reason I showed up."

I promised.

At the end of the clinic, the lady, leading her horse, came up to me. I heard the panic rising in her voice.

"Clinton, Clinton, before you leave, you promised me that you would work with my horse's right front foot."

"Sure," I said, "No problem. Why don't you try to pick his foot up now and show me what he does?"

Left: 7.1 **Whatever you might think your horse's problem is, it is probably not that simple. Chances are what you're seeing is really just a symptom of an underlying cause.**

The lady looked at me, kind of disgusted. "He's only going to rear up and strike out."

"I'm sure he will," I said, "but just humor me anyway and let me see what he does."

Reluctantly, she bent over and picked up the horse's right front foot. The horse just stood there like an old pony.

The lady was at first shocked—and then she got mad. "I can't believe he's doing this!"

"Aren't you happy that he's standing there, nice and relaxed, and not rearing up?"

"Well, yes, but he's just doing it because you're standing here," she said.

I tried not to smile. "Okay," I said. "Maybe you got lucky. Let's try again and see what he does."

She bent over and picked up the horse's right front foot, and again, he stood there like a statue. Didn't move a muscle. This made her really mad.

"I can't believe he's doing this!" she said again, her voice shrill with exasperation. "I don't know what's going on."

"I thought you wanted this to get fixed," I said.

She glared at me. "I do want it to get fixed, but I don't know how we fixed it, and if you leave here today, and he starts rearing in the air again next week, I won't know what to do about it."

"Ma'am, what have we been working on with groundwork for the last three days?" I asked.

She thought for a moment. "Getting the horse respectful."

"That's right," I said. "And not only have we been working on getting the horse respectful, but we've also been working on getting the fear out of him. We've been sensitizing and desensitizing to pressure, moving your horse's feet forward, backward, left, and right, rewarding the slightest try, and getting him respectful on the ground and under saddle.

"So now, three days later, when you pick up his front foot, he doesn't give you any of the usual problems. Why?" I paused for a second, and then answered my own question. "Because we got his respect without fear."

I looked at the horse. "You never had a right front foot problem. You had a lack of respect problem that just happened to show up in his right front foot."

This lesson illustrates one of the hardest things for me to get across to people. Whatever you think your horse's problem is, chances are, it is really *not* the problem. This is something I didn't understand in the beginning either, but once I started developing my knowledge through both Gordon and Ian's programs, it became evident that horse problems aren't problems per se, but they're really just symptoms of an underlying cause.

For those of you who have never been to one of my horsemanship clinics, we do groundwork as a group until lunch, then afterward we ride as a group. Until lunch we work on moving the horse's feet forward, backward, left, and right—and getting the horse soft and supple and paying attention. The reason why I don't let anybody ride before lunch is because the groundwork is what keeps everybody safe. In fact, I don't let anybody ride unless I think that they're going to survive the experience. I have 20 to 30 people in every clinic, so my top priority is to do my very best to keep people from being injured.

If I had tried to pick up that horse's foot on Friday morning when the lady first asked me to, what do you think the horse would have done? I guarantee he would have reared up and struck out. He would have done to me exactly what he did to her.

I don't think that she was lying or exaggerating at all. Why didn't I try to work with him Friday morning? Because I knew it was a waste of my time. I knew that horse didn't have a foot problem. All that had been ruled out. What he had was a lack of respect and some fear issues that just happened to show up in his right front foot.

99.9 percent of horse problems come from fear or lack of respect—or both

I wish I had a dollar for every time someone has said, "Clinton, my horse bites me." A horse that bites is a problem, for sure, but biting is nothing more than another symptom of the same cause—disrespect. Once you get the horse respectful, he'll no longer want to bite you.

Another thing I hear often is, "Clinton, my horse wants to buck with a saddle on." In most cases when a horse wants to buck with a saddle, it's because he's fearful. Once you get the horse comfortable wearing the saddle and you get the fear out of him, usually the horse doesn't want to buck anymore (photos 7.2 A & B).

You might say, "Clinton, how am I supposed to know if the problems are coming from fear or a lack of respect? What do I do about this?"

7.2 A **Most problems, such as this kind of reaction on the lunge line, come from fear or lack of respect—and sometimes both! The good news is that my Method addresses both these underlying causes with the same solution: moving the horse's feet.**

7.2 B **In most cases, when a horse bucks like this when a saddle has been placed on his back, it's because he's frightened of it. Once he gets comfortable wearing it, he usually won't buck anymore. After the first saddling, I don't let a horse buck. Instead, when he starts to, I make him do lots of changes in direction to redirect his energy.**

LESSONS WELL LEARNED

7.3 **Remember: whatever the horse's problem, the solution is almost always to move his feet—forward, backward, left, and right. I'm backing this horse up using steady pressure to correct a mistake. You have about three seconds to correct a horse by moving his feet, and backing him up aggressively is one of the easiest and best ways I know of to get the point across.**

The answer is that you don't have to know when you begin *where* your problem is coming from.

By following my program step-by-step—on the ground and in the saddle—you will inevitably discover the real reason behind your horse's problem. For example, if your horse has a lack of respect, as soon as you start to do the groundwork exercises and move his feet, he'll get resentful and challenge you. You'll know when you see that happen that his problem is a lack of respect. And, if you try to desensitize your horse with the rope and the Handy Stick and String, and he comes unglued and has a heart attack, you'll know that a lot of your problem issues originate from fear.

Even if you don't know where your problem is coming from, as long as you do the groundwork exercises and move your horse's feet, you are teaching your horse to respect you and to use the "thinking"—as opposed to the "reactive"—side of his brain (photo 7.3).

When you do desensitizing exercises, you work on getting the fear out of your horse so that he will no longer be scared by objects that move and make noise. That's the beautiful thing about my program. Because I've numbered, categorized, and laid out all the exercises step-by-step, both on the ground and under saddle, all you have to do is have enough dedication to follow them.

In the process of completing the entire series of exercises, you'll solve whatever problems—and causes of problems—you have. Remember, whatever horse problems you think you have, these are most often *not* the problem, but rather a symptom of an underlying cause.

Lesson 8

Horses for courses and people for horses

It's as important to find the right job for your horse as it is to choose the right horse for the job that you want him to do.

THE

two-year-old I was riding did not have one ounce of "stop" in him whatsoever. This is something great reining horses either love to do or won't do at all. Sure, you can teach all of them to stop moving forward, but you can't teach them to really "get down and get gritty." And unfortunately, if a reining horse won't slide to a stop, you aren't going to beat anybody in the show pen.

The horses I raise and train for competition are genetically bred to be outstanding reining horses. This horse was by a great reining sire and out of great reining mare, but even though he was bred and raised for high-end reining competition, I'd come to realize that he would be much happier doing something else. So what would I do? I'd sell this horse to someone as a trail riding horse, a team penning horse, or for some other event at which he'd excel.

My observations of horses and people through the years have taught me a valuable lesson that has proved itself time and again. This lesson has also led to one of my favorite sayings—something I think everyone involved in any way with horses should live by: "Horses for courses and people for horses."

What does this mean? It means that, just like this two-year-old I was riding, not every horse is going to suit every course. The second part of this lesson is that not every person is right for every horse. In my clinics, I watch a lot of different kinds of people interact with a lot of different kinds of horses. Through countless observations over the years, I

Left: 8.1 **While you can teach all horses to stop moving forward, you can't teach them to really "get down and get gritty" like Sparkles is doing here. This is something great reining horses love to do. Some horses won't do it at all.**

have discovered that to be safe and get the best result, people need to complement their horses, not match them.

For example, a jittery, type-A person on a hot, nervous horse is a recipe for disaster. But, put a type-A on a more laid-back horse, and this person will just naturally do a good job of keeping the horse's feet moving. On the other hand, a laid-back person on a laid-back horse will be frustrated by the horse's growing disrespect and lack of responsiveness, but the same rider on a hot, nervous horse will have a more calming influence and not override or do things that make the horse even more spooky.

Horses for courses

Just because you want a horse to do something—a specific discipline or event—doesn't mean that he is bred to do it. Or, even if he is bred to do it, that doesn't mean that he wants to do it. Horses, just like kids, have their own unique personality. It doesn't matter how much you want them to act a certain way, they're going to follow whatever their personality type dictates. You can certainly mold them and help things along, but each horse is born with his own unique characteristics (photo 8.2).

8.2 **Just because you want a horse to do something—and just because he is bred to do it—doesn't mean he'll want to. All horses are individuals and their personality, temperament, and preferences vary just like ours do. Look at how my horse is tuned in to the cow—this is a horse that obviously loves his job.**

The first thing I tell people to do when they're looking for a horse is to buy one that is suited for the course they want it to follow (photos 8.3 A & B). For example, if you're going to do endurance riding that requires a lot of athletic ability and stamina, I'd recommend that you buy an Arab—a horse that is bred to cover a lot of miles in an efficient manner. For this particular course, I would not choose a Belgian draft horse. They are bred to be big, strong, stout, and pull heavy loads, but they're slow. Could I do a 30-mile endurance ride on a Belgian draft horse? Of course I could—but it would take me three years to finish the ride!

8.3 A & B **No matter how well a horse is bred and trained, you have to look at what's he's going to be happiest doing. When a horse loves the trails more than the arena, he's going to make a much better, more dependable partner for a trail rider than he would be for someone whose heart is set on competing.**

If you're going to trail ride once a week and you don't have a lot of time to spend with your horse, I wouldn't recommend buying an athletic, hot-blooded horse like an Arab or a Thoroughbred. That's like taking a Border Collie into the city and giving it a 20-foot backyard. He goes crazy. But if you take that dog to a cattle ranch and give him 200 to 300 acres to run around on, he's the greatest dog in the world because he's got room to exert all that energy.

So if you're just going to ride once a week or once every other week, choose a more cold-blooded breed of horse. These kinds of horses dream about sleeping and don't *want* to be ridden every day. At the same time, if you *do* want to ride every day and be a little bit more athletic, I'd choose more of a hot-blooded horse.

Try to buy a horse that already knows what you want him to do. If you want to trail ride, buy a horse that is already being successfully and frequently ridden on the trails. If you buy a young, two-year-old green filly that has only been out on the trail once—and only at a walk—you're just asking for trouble.

If what you need is a kids' horse, buy one from a family that has kids roughly the same types and ages as your own. There's no point buying a kids' horse that has been ridden by a 13-year-old boy if you want one for your four-year-old girl. Usually, a girl of this age wants something that's going to be quiet and safe, and a 13-year-old boy just wants to go fast. And, just because a horse is a good adult horse doesn't mean that it's going to make a good kids' horse.

So for the best result when buying, first look for a horse that is already suited for the course that you want to pursue. If you have a horse that doesn't suit a particular discipline, try to find a type of riding that he will suit, or sell him to someone who is looking for a horse with his particular strengths. This way both you and the horse have a chance to be happy doing what you want to do.

People for horses

Just like not every horse is suited to every course, not every person suits every horse. You want to find a horse whose temperament complements—and is a balance for—your personality. Because horses, like people, have their own personalities, there will be some horses, just like some people, that you just may not like. There's no fun in working with horses you don't click with. That doesn't mean you can't train them or ride them, but when I get a horse I don't like, I sell him. And nine times out of 10, the person I sell such a horse to absolutely loves him (photos 8.4 A–D).

Horses teach people and people teach horses

One of the most frustrating things I deal with in clinics is the person who chooses something like a Mustang as her first horse. Or, the one who falls in love with a big, beautiful hot-blooded horse, and then proceeds to try to learn to ride on that horse. Or, the parents who buy a young horse for their kid so they can "grow up together." A green horse and a green rider trying to learn together is nothing more than a classic recipe for disaster.

When you're first learning how to ride, choose a horse that is going to teach *you* how to ride—a horse with a lot of experience and plenty of miles under his feet. That will build your confidence. Once you develop your own feel, timing, and experience, you can buy a greener horse that doesn't know very much, and then you can teach the horse. Remember: horses teach people, and *then* people teach horses.

8.4 A–D **Remember: "Horses for courses, and people for horses." These women have very different horses, very different personalities and very different courses, yet they all have one thing in common: they have each chosen a horse that suits both what they want to do with him and their personality. Brenda loves trail riding on Buddy, a paint Tennessee Walker; Betty loves a variety of riding and training activities with "Butch," a bay Arabian.**

Teresa shows Lladro, a Friesian, at high levels of dressage competition.

Linden, shown here riding "Speedy," has enjoyed riding and showing cutting horses for most of her life.

Sherri, who also grew up riding and showing horses, is now sharing this love with her children with the help of Pearl, a 16-year-old retired jumper who still holds her own in a variety of show events.

Lesson 9

Take everything step-by-step

Frustration, obstacles, and challenges in horse training —
and in life — are best overcome by staying focused,
finding balance, and taking things one step at a time.

THE *California August sun blazed down on the portable fence arena set up for my clinic in the middle of a cow pasture. But it wasn't the 110-degree heat and sweltering humidity that was making my blood boil. It was this woman who, for the past two-and-a-half days of my three-day clinic, had been annoying everyone there—including me—with her incessant whining and complaining. And now she was in my face again.*

"Cliiiiiintoooooon, my horse won't dooooo this." She stood there with her hand on her hip. "Will you come over here and help meeeee??????"

Every time she said it, my name had WAY too many syllables. I wasn't sure I was going to be able to be nice to her for one more minute. In fact, I realized that if I didn't get away from this woman within the next 20 seconds, I was going to say or do something I would seriously regret.

I bit my tongue. I smiled. "Can you excuse me for just a minute?" I somehow managed to say without snarling. "I need to go to the restroom. I'll be right back."

I heard her "harrumph" as I walked away, but I did not slow down. I walked as fast as I could all the way to the lone porta-potty brought in for the clinic. I pulled open the door and, fighting my way through the blast of stench and the swarm of blowflies that greeted me, I went in, closed the toilet lid and sat down with my head in my hands. To my complete surprise, I just started to sob.

Left: 9.1 **My goal is always to make it as easy as possible for horses and their owners to get along. In my tour demonstrations, such as this one in Abilene, Texas, I provide tangible, easy-to-follow examples that make sense to both owner and horse. In these tour stops, I seek to inspire people to achieve better communication with their horse.**

"No amount of money is worth this," I said to the blowflies. I was just feeling so sorry for myself. I was literally sitting in the most horrible, disgusting place I could imagine. Flies were getting in my nose and sweat mixed with tears was dripping off my face. Basically, I was having a mental breakdown in the toilet!

After about five minutes of this, I wiped off my face and said to myself, "Okay, Clinton, you're going to pick yourself up and you're going to walk out of this stinking toilet and you're going to go back over there and smile at that woman and help her as if she's your best friend. And you're going to get through this weekend. From now on, you're not going to look at the whole year; you're just going to focus on one week at a time. You're going to get through this year because you made a commitment—but you're never going to book 48 clinics in one year again."

It had been a hell of a year. When I first came to the United States, I didn't have any money. I started Downunder Horsemanship with less than $1,000 and I took on every opportunity I could. I did clinics every single weekend and from Monday to Thursday each week, I trained five to six horses. I had agreed to do 48 clinics this particular year, and the other four weekends were committed to filming DVDs.

I was worn out and it was only August. I felt like my eyes were hanging out of my head and my hands were hanging down to my feet. I looked like a burned-out rat.

9.2 **Training people is far more demanding, mentally and physically, than training horses. In my Horsemanship Clinics, I provide step-by-step instruction to build skills and confidence for both horse and rider. Here I am helping a woman teach her horse to flex to the halter.**

LESSONS WELL LEARNED

What I had also realized was that it is far harder to teach people than it is to teach horses. When I'm training a horse, I know what I'm doing—I'm just getting the job done. But when you're trying to get somebody else to do it who either doesn't know how to or isn't physically capable, it can be very frustrating at times. And, while teaching people can certainly have its rewards, I hadn't counted on how mentally and physically demanding it would be (photo 9.2).

9.3 A & B **To stay motivated and meet the demands of a packed tour and clinic schedule, I've learned to stay focused on the moment, the experience, and the city I'm in. My secretary hands me a plane ticket and that's where I go. In life, just like when training horses, it is important to take things one step at a time.**

The importance of balance and moderation

The lesson in the porta-potty provided me with a valuable insight on the importance of balance and moderation, which has stuck with me ever since. To this day, I do not look at my full schedule, but instead only look at one week in advance. When people walk up to me and ask where I'm going to be in two months, I really have no idea. Each week my secretary hands me a ticket, and I just go there (photos 9.3 A & B).

One of the hardest things to do for anyone who teaches for a living, when you have to repeat the exact same information week after week, is to stay motivated. The way I stay motivated is to stay focused on the moment I'm in: one step at a time, one clinic at a time, one filming segment at a time, and one city at a time.

The lesson also taught me that while you do have to work hard to get ahead in life, money really can't buy you happiness. A lot of people will hear that and say, "Yeah, right." But it's really true. Because even though I did make a good chunk of change that year when I did 48 clinics, it wasn't worth the misery felt when I was crying in the toilet (photo 9.4).

I was raised with a tremendous work ethic that I am thankful for—even in his sixties, my dad still works from 4:00 A.M. to 6:00 P.M. six days a week. Combining that influence with my natural tendency to bite off

9.4 **On this day in a 48-clinic year, I learned the hard way that balance and moderation are the keys to sanity. I hope you never need to escape to a porta-potty as I did to learn this lesson!**

9.5 A–C **I also stay motivated by learning new things and stepping up to new challenges in my own horsemanship. The "Road to the Horse" colt-starting championship gave me a chance to successfully use my Method in head-to-head competition against two other top trainers. In less than three hours, we had to teach an untrained horse to be ridden. I also love to show in reining, cow-horse, and cutting competitions. I feel it keeps me humble and eager to improve my own riding skills. Despite a rigorous tour and clinic schedule, I still manage to train and show at the highest levels of competition.**

more than I can chew, I created my own imbalance that I have since tried to correct with a little more moderation. While I still do whatever it takes to get the job done, I'm constantly trying to find that healthy middle ground between working myself to death and not getting out of bed all day. Whereas before I felt like a lazy bum if I took a day off, as I get older, I'm learning that it's all right to take off one day a week.

So to get ahead, in life and with horses, you have to work hard, go out and grab what you want with your own two hands, and stay motivated (photos 9.5 A–C). If you can find that balance for yourself, mate, you may be able to find a better escape from life's stressors than a stinking, blowfly-infested porta-potty on a hot August day.

Lesson 10

To change your horse, you must first change yourself

Being willing to open your mind, increase your knowledge, gain experience, and make a commitment to consistent effort will first transform you — and then your horse.

"CLINTON,

have you ever met a horse you couldn't train?" The man standing before me was asking the same question I've been asked probably a million times. "I've really tried, but I can't seem to do anything with my horse. I'm starting to think maybe he can't change."

My answer to this question was the same as it always was: "No, but I've met a million people that don't want to be trained."

The one thing most people realize about me is that I'm going to tell you the truth. Now, I may not always tell you exactly what you want to hear, but I'll always tell you the truth. "Sir," I said, looking him squarely in the eye, "If you want a horse to change, you have to be willing to change yourself first."

"Change how?" he asked.

"Well, if your horse is going well and behaving himself, it is because you are doing a good job training him," I explained. "But if your horse is being disrespectful, acting spooky, jumpy, and going badly, it means you are doing a poor job of training him."

People generally hate to hear me say this because it puts all the responsibility back on them. This man, however, took the news fairly well, and he persisted. "But I bought this horse with all these problems," he explained.

"I'm sorry," I said, "but if you wrote the check, they're your problems now. Even if you didn't cause or create these problems, they're yours to deal with. To change your horse's behavior, you have

Left: 10.1 **The people who come to my tours and clinics are obviously willing to change themselves. That's why I know they'll be successful in changing their horse.**

to change how you are interacting with him. If you just keep doing the same things, you're just going to keep getting the same results. If you want something different, change what you're doing."

"Oh, okay," he said, turning to go.

"But hey, mate, the good news is that you're here, so that means you're willing to try something different," I said. He had stood in line for a while to ask his question, so obviously it was important to him. I hated him to feel as if I had given him too short an answer for his big problem, but the answer really was just that simple.

I gestured around me at the 10,000-seat arena, of which about 4,500 seats were occupied. "Do you see all those empty seats up there?"

He looked around, a little confused. "Yes." He clearly had no idea where I was going with this.

"When I look up at those empty seats," I said, "to me every empty seat represents a horse owner in this state who is really unhappy about how his horse rides, performs, and acts, but is unwilling to do anything about it. People who tell me their horse won't change are almost always the ones who are unwilling to change themselves."

Ian Francis used to have a little saying, "To change your life, you must first change your attitude." I put my own little spin on that, saying, "To change your horse, you must first change yourself."

The simple truth of this lesson I first learned from Ian has proved itself to me almost as many times as I have answered the question about whether any horse can be trained. When people want to change their horse's behavior, and they demonstrate this desire by increasing their knowledge, one of my greatest rewards is first, watching the transformation in the person, and second, seeing that change reflected in the horse's behavior.

That's why I always say, "When you come to my tours and seminars, come with an open mind. Come with a willingness to learn." Just because you're learning a new way to interact with your horse doesn't mean that it's going to be easy. However, if you're passionate about learning and have a desire to change, as a result, your skills will get better; your feel, timing, and experience will improve; and all this will lead to a better relationship between you and your horse (photo 10.2). And likewise, if you are not willing to change yourself first, whatever it is about your horse that is giving you problems will most likely continue.

10.2 **The more you learn and hone your horsemanship skills, the more your confidence will improve, too. This young woman is flexing her horse to the halter before saddling. Just a few minutes of groundwork before you ride will help ensure a safer, more pleasurable experience.**

Three ways to get a horse trained

Another thing I tell people who aren't happy with their horse is that there are just three ways to get a horse trained: buy him trained; pay someone to train him; or train him yourself. If you don't want to put in the effort to train a horse or you don't know how to, you can buy a horse that is already trained or pay someone to train him. But even when you buy a horse that's already trained or have your horse trained by someone else, if you don't do the right things to keep him respectful toward you, over time that horse will get worse and worse and worse.

Your horse isn't going to get trained—or stay trained—sitting in his stall. He's not going to get broke—or stay broke—standing out in the pasture. Every minute you are with your horse, whether you realize it or not, you are either training him or *un*-training him. If you aren't happy with what your horse is doing or how he is behaving, you have to take the time to learn how to interact with him differently so that you can use whatever time you spend with him to change the behavior you don't like.

Just as your children don't learn the values and lessons you want them to learn in life by sitting in front of the TV or computer, you have to teach your horses what you want them to know. And just like you have to allow your children to make mistakes so they can learn from them, you have to learn how to let your horse make a mistake—and then correct that mistake—to bring about the progress you want. With children and with horses, you have to be willing to spend quality time with them if you want them to grow.

10.3 **I still consult Ian Francis as often as I can to keep refining and expanding my knowledge and understanding about training horses. Here Ian and I are taking a ride together after working these horses in the arena so we can discuss their progress. No matter how much I learn, I always want to know more!**

Constant learning means continuous improvement

Just as I advise the people who come to my tours and clinics to come with an open mind and always seek more knowledge and new ways to improve, I, too, am still constantly trying to learn. I fly Ian Francis over to the United States every single year for two weeks to work with him, to continue to learn from him, and for him to personally work with my horses (photo 10.3). I've brought Gordon over as well, and I go back to Australia to study with both of them every chance I get.

Every morning when I get up, I spend half an hour watching DVDs of Ian and Gordon while I eat my breakfast, going over and over what they've taught me, constantly trying to keep getting better (photo 10.4). I love to learn from anybody.

I probably own something—books, articles, or DVDs—from just about every major horse trainer or clinician in the world. Sometimes I agree with what I see, and it reassures me that I'm on the right track, and sometimes when I disagree with what I see, I know for *sure* I'm on the right track. Although about 95 percent of the time I don't see anything new, I'd say that about 5 percent of the time, I see something I haven't considered, and I want to expand on these ideas and work with them a little bit.

Because of this passion for continuous learning, what I'm doing today as a clinician is so much better than what I was doing several years ago. I'd be willing to bet that five years from today, whatever I'm doing as a teacher will be that much better than what I'm doing today.

As a result of my willingness to keep changing myself, I am able to continue improving the changes I can bring about in my horses. This opportunity is there for you, too, mate. You just have to open yourself to it and be willing to do the work it takes to get there. The results, I promise you, are well worth the trouble.

10.4 **Every morning while I eat my breakfast, I watch my lessons with Ian Francis. Continuous study is how I stay sharp in my own horsemanship journey.**

Lesson 11

To be effective, you have to be understood

Black-and-white communication with horses creates the understanding that helps solve problems and paves the way for achieving your highest goals.

HE was a great big, lazy, 16.3-hand, 1,250-pound, Thoroughbred-draft cross and the petite woman at the other end of his lead rope was about 120 pounds dripping wet with rocks in her pockets.

We had just started a clinic and after I demonstrated the first back-up exercise, she tapped the air in front of the horse to ask him to back up. The horse ignored her. But instead of increasing the pressure as I had instructed, she just kept it the same, asking her horse to back up over and over at the same pressure level. The horse continued to ignore her. I watched for a while and after about five minutes of this, her horse actually stepped forward and tried to bite her.

I decided it was time to intervene. "Do you know why he just tried to bite you?" I asked, taking the stick from her hand.

"No," she said, bewildered. "I don't."

"He tried to bite you because you are annoying him too much."

This took her aback. "What do you mean?"

"To be effective you have to be understood," I told her.

I tapped the air with rhythm: one-two-three-four. The horse didn't budge. I increased the pressure, tapping the rope: one-two-three-four. No response, so I increased the pressure. I started whacking the rope, one-two-three-four, and then whacked the clip, but still the horse would not back up. I ended up actually whacking this horse right on the nose—and in response, he backed up two steps.

I kept repeating the exercise, gradually turning up the heat

Left: 11.1 **When you let a horse get pushy and disrespectful, it's only a matter of time before you get seriously hurt. This young woman is allowing her horse to crowd into her personal space; what she needs to do is teach him to stay out of her personal "hula hoop," unless she invites him in this close.**

every four counts until the horse backed up a couple of steps. After about 10 more minutes, the horse backed up as soon as I tapped the air—just like the lady was doing when she started out. I handed her back the stick. "Do you see now what I mean?" I asked.

"Yes," she said, looking troubled. "But I really didn't like you whacking him on the nose."

"I didn't like that either," I said. "I'm all for you being gentle with your horse, but you have to be willing to do whatever it takes to get the job done! You always start out as easy as possible, but you have to be willing to get as firm as necessary to get your point across."

In the very same clinic I observed a large man working with his Thoroughbred-Arab cross mare. She was very athletic, very sensitive—and absolutely terrified of him.

I watched them for a few minutes, and every time he asked her to back up he started out by whacking the lead rope—hard. In response, she'd rear, spin around, and jump out of her skin. Her eyes were huge and terrified with white showing all around.

I stepped forward and took the stick out of his hand. "Why do you think she's reacting that way?" I asked, glad to give the poor horse a break.

"I don't know," he grumbled. "She just doesn't get that I want her to back up, I guess."

"No," I said, taking the lead rope from him. "What's happening here is you're pressuring her too much. She can't even think about backing up because you're scaring her to death by applying way too much pressure. You have to start by gently tapping the air, using rhythm, and then give her a chance to back up."

I showed him what I meant. Immediately, the filly relaxed and took two steps back. I handed him back the stick and lead rope. "As easy as possible," I said, stressing the other end of the pressure spectrum, "but as firm as necessary. And always reward the slightest try."

What this lesson all comes down to is being effective in our communication with horses. Throughout the years I've learned how to help people learn to use body language and pressure effectively to achieve more black-and-white communication with their horses—and exactly *how* to use these kinds of communication to get the results they're looking for.

11.2 A–D **To be effective you must first be understood; you have to develop a feel for how much pressure to use, when to increase it and when to release it. In the first two photos, this horse is ignoring his owner who is trying—ineffectively—to back him up.**

In these photos, I demonstrate how to get the point across first by tapping the air, then tapping the lead rope. Since the horse does not back up, I then proceed to whack the rope. This action has definitely got this horse's attention. Now when she asks her horse to back up just by tapping the air, he does so right away. By always starting with the lightest amount of pressure, you will teach your horse to respond to that pressure. This avoids your having to "turn up the heat." Whether you need to light a fire under your horse's feet or just barely tap the air, you've got to be able to assess the horse's background, temperament, and the situation in order to get the job done.

I typically encounter two kinds of people in my clinics and both of them have the same problem—although they come at it from completely opposite directions.

One group, which I call the "Nagging Mothers Association," just nags and nags and nags at their horses but doesn't ever increase the pressure enough to get the job done (photos 11.2 A–D).

11.3 A–C **As this man puts way too much pressure on his horse when asking her to back up, she in turn reacts badly.**

The other group, which I call the "Barbarians Association," tends to start with high levels of pressure and doesn't ever give their horse a chance to make the right decision before they turn up the heat even more (photos 11.3 A–C).

When we start the groundwork exercises, I have found that men often tend to be more on the Barbarian side and women are often more inclined to be on the Nagging Mothers side. What would be ideal is a combination of these traits—tempering the goal-oriented, structured aggression of a man with the sensitivity, intuition, and feel that women more naturally have.

In addition to monitoring your own behavior, you've also got to learn to assess the horse, his temperament, his background, and the situation in order to get the job done. Whether you need to light a fire under your horse's feet or just barely touch the air, people have to learn to adjust their behavior to fit the situation. That's why I say horses are nothing more than professional people trainers.

When I take over and ask with just a little bit of pressure, I get a much better result. You've got to read the situation to know how much pressure to apply.

Now that the owner is applying the right amount of pressure, the horse is doing exactly what he wants.

11.4 A **This lady is "sneaking around" her horse too much. Here she is trying to sneak the lead rope up over the horse's back instead of being direct and obvious when exposing him to it.**

Horses read body language first

Because body language is a horse's primary mode of communication, it is what a horse will pick up on first. When people learn to get black-and-white with their body language, they start to communicate with their horse the way horses communicate with each other. Active body language means "Move now!" Passive body language means, "Stand still and relax." When you really start to pay attention to what your body language is saying to your horse, you'll be amazed at how quickly and dramatically your results will improve (photos 11.4 A & B).

People sometimes ask me about using verbal cues, saying they'd rather use verbal cues with their horses. I tell them that verbal cues are okay, as long as they remember that verbal cues are not a horse's primary mode of communication, and for this reason are probably not going to be all that effective.

I've also noticed that people who use more verbal cues tend to pay less attention to their body language, and sometimes this confuses the

11.4 B **I'm using very active body language to get this horse to move his feet. Notice how I'm leaning forward, looking at his hindquarters, and being very direct. The more you exaggerate your body language the easier it is for your horse to understand what you want him to do.**

horse. Remember, any time a shade of gray exists in your communication you set your horse up for failure. For a horse, a shade of gray is a place where he doesn't know whether he is right or wrong.

Be as gentle as possible, but as firm as necessary

In addition to helping people learn how to be black-and-white in their communication with their horse, I teach them how to "be as gentle as possible, but as firm as necessary, and always to reward the slightest try." By starting gently, we give the horse several chances to find the right answer. He may ignore you at first, but as you gradually increase the pressure, it gets harder and harder for him to ignore you, and it forces him to look for a new answer. When a horse finally says, "Okay, Clinton, I just can't ignore you anymore," and tries—even though his first try may not be perfect—I reward that effort. That's what I mean by "always reward the slightest try."

I see a lot of Nagging Mothers making the mistake of never turning up the pressure. When a horse is ignoring you and you never turn up the heat, there is no motive for him to do anything different. If you never make a horse feel uncomfortable for choosing the wrong behavior, why would he want to look for another answer?

And, if you threaten and don't follow through, your horse has called your bluff and you have lost his respect. Once he learns that you won't follow through, his behavior will only get worse.

Just remember: horses don't learn from the pressure, but rather, from the *release* of pressure. Pressure is what motivates the horse to look for another answer. Releasing the pressure tells him he did the right thing. And when you use pressure in this way, his behavior is always his choice.

With enough repetition and consistency, he'll make the right behavior a habit. Building these right behaviors one at a time is what makes my Method so successful and easy for people to use.

Driving pressure vs. steady pressure

Another thing I try to help people understand through specific exercises, both on the ground and in the saddle, is how to use two different types of pressure—driving pressure and steady pressure—to get the result they want.

Driving pressure, which is applied with a one-two-three-four rhythm, is uncomfortable to a horse. To be effective, you must be willing to stay with that same rhythm, turning up the heat with each four-count until you get the response you're looking for. Then when you stop, that release of pressure teaches the horse, "THIS is the response I want, and I will accept nothing less." Once a horse makes the right choice and he recognizes it is right because it is when you stopped the driving pressure, from then on, it takes less and less driving pressure to get the same response.

Steady pressure, on the other hand, doesn't work as well at first, because horses like to lean into steady pressure. They can do it all day. Think about Sumo wrestlers pushing each other around the ring. That's steady pressure. When you use steady pressure with a horse, you're starting a shoving match with a 1,000-pound animal—and you'll lose every time.

With driving pressure, on the other hand, a horse can't get hold of you long enough to lean on you, so eventually he'll give up and move what you are asking him to move. The use of steady pressure comes later in a horse's training as you start refining behavior under saddle, building on the exercises—and the responsiveness—the horse first learned from the ground.

There's no substitute for hands-on experience

Gaining the knowledge is only part of it. Once you understand a general principle, you have to get hands-on practice and experience with different horses to get really good at it. Horses are a lot like children—they're products of the environment they've grown up in. You have to realize that in addition to temperament, you're also dealing with patterns already established. For this reason, every horse you work with will show you a slightly different application of the general principle you first learned. With each horse you work with, you'll understand how the principle works even better.

I learned most of what I know in my first four years of study. I've spent the last 18 years practicing what I learned with different horses and getting more effective at it. To be understood by your horse, you have to be effective in your communication with him. To be effective takes experience and awareness, and that only comes with practice.

People worry about messing up their horses when they are learning—about doing the wrong things or confusing the horse. And yes, that will happen sometimes. But horses are very forgiving creatures, and even if you don't get it exactly right at first, as you keep on learning you can fix whatever you mess up in the beginning. I suppose that's why we all love horses so much—they truly know how to forgive!

Lesson 12

The way to earn a horse's respect is by moving his feet

Responding to challenges in the horse's own language will keep you in the driver's seat — and at the top of the pecking order in your herd of two.

THE

big stallion eyed me as I entered his stall. It was one of my first jobs in the United States, and I had been warned about this horse. There was even an axe handle with a string through it hanging outside his stall just for the purpose of defending oneself against his attacks.

"These are not just love bites we're talking about," the head trainer had advised me as he showed me the axe handle on my first day on the job. "If he gets hold of you, he'll toss you around like a rag doll."

Needless to say, I didn't take my eyes off this horse as I cleaned his stall. I watched as others tried to handle him, and they'd beat him with that axe handle every time he tried to bite them. They always saddled him in cross-ties so he couldn't bite them.

I had some ideas about what would fix him, but this outfit didn't think too much of natural horsemanship and groundwork and all that. This was a show barn and all they really cared about was what this horse did under saddle—they were concerned only with showing and winning.

After I had been there about a month, the trainer left for a week to go to a show. My job while he was gone was to work with this horse every day. As soon as they left, I decided I was going to try to do something about the stallion's bad behavior.

First, I put him in the round pen, and I piled the brushes and the saddle in the center. I had my own halter and lead rope on him, and every time he tried to bite me as I brushed him, I'd lunge

Left: 12.1 **Backing your horse up is one of the best groundwork exercises you can do. A horse that backs well on the ground is showing you a lot of respect.**

him—really hustle his feet for about five minutes or so, and then, as if nothing had happened, I'd just start brushing him again.

The next time he tried to bite me, I aggressively backed him around the round pen three or four times. Then I just went back to brushing him. After the third or fourth time of his trying to bite me and having his feet moved until he was huffing and puffing for air, he realized that as long as he kept his lips to himself, he got to stand still.

I saddled him the same way, right in the center of that round pen, hustling his feet anytime he tried to bite me. After two days of going through the same thing with him as I just brushed and saddled him, he was standing still, head held low, hind leg cocked—as docile as a lamb.

Next I started doing a little extra groundwork with him, Yielding the Hindquarters, Sidepassing, Lungeing for Respect, and as I did, he just grew more and more docile and acted less and less like a stud. By the end of the week, I was saddling him in the barn aisle, with mares all around us. I'd brush, saddle, clean his feet, and he never even flinched, never tried to bite, never even acted like he noticed the mares.

Of course, when the trainer and his staff returned I couldn't tell them what I had done. So I just waited and watched. As the trainer saddled him, he just stood there, not misbehaving one bit. The trainer said, "I guess that axe handle finally worked! I knew it would if we just kept at it."

I said nothing. The next question on my mind was how many days would it take before this horse would be back to his old behavior? For the next two days, he was a complete angel. Then on the third day, he turned and gave a cranky look at the girl who was saddling him. Seeing this look, she immediately whacked him with the lead rope.

I actually saw the light come on in this horse's mind, as if to say, "Oh! I remember this program!" In two more days this horse was completely back to his old disagreeable self.

What did this lesson teach me? You can't demand a horse's respect. You have to earn it. And you do that by moving his feet. What I had done to turn this old stallion's attitude around had worked as long as he thought the person handling him was worthy of his respect. If, when he had given that girl the cranky look, she had moved his feet by back-

12.2 **It's very important for a horse to establish his place in the pecking order within the herd. It is just as important to establish the pecking order between you and your horse. Remember: You're the leader and he's the follower.**

ing him up and down the aisle instead of whacking him on the nose, he'd most likely have gone back to being an angel.

Even with a horse that is very well trained, if you don't maintain that level of respect, the horse is going to get a little worse every day. And while what I did carried over somewhat to the other people working with the stallion, the minute he tested them, they showed him that they didn't have the same program as I did, and therefore did not merit the same respect.

So while respect doesn't automatically carry over from one individual to the next, it can be maintained if people tend to do the same types of things.

To establish the pecking order in a herd, horses ask each other the very same question they ask of us to determine whether we are worthy of their respect: "Do you know how to move my feet?" (photo 12.2). And, if not, let the games begin! So remember, with horses the one who moves the other's feet always wins.

Why punishment doesn't work with horses

A lot of people don't realize that punishment doesn't work with horses because they're prey animals. When you punish a prey animal, he just gets frightened of you. Because horses can't learn when they're frightened, they don't learn through punishment. When you punish a horse, he gets all upset, runs backward, and is so consumed with fear that he can't think about anything else.

However, when you move a horse's feet until he feels uncomfortable, he can understand the correction because his brain isn't occupied with fear.

Punishment, on the other hand works well with predators. Dogs—and husbands—learn from punishment because they're predators. You can punish a dog, "Bad Dog!" and he cowers down as if to say "I'm sorry, I won't do that again." Or, "Bad Husband!" and the response is usually "I'm sorry, honey, I won't do that again."

When horses kick and bite each other, it doesn't frighten them because they're the same species. Have you ever noticed that horses can kick and bite each other and then five minutes later be standing side by side under a tree, swishing flies off each other? However, when we chase and hit our horse it terrifies him because we are not the same species. We're predators, and they're prey animals, and this difference means that instead of learning from punishment, they just get frightened.

Also, keep in mind that when a horse misbehaves, you have three seconds to correct the mistake. I call this the "Three Second Rule." After three seconds, you might as well forget it because they will not connect the correction with the mistake. Say a horse bites me. If I don't move his feet within three seconds, moving his feet is a waste of time. If I lunge him or back him up after even four or five seconds, he won't know what he's getting in trouble for (photos 12.3 A–D). Of course, in some circumstances, such as when your horse is in crossties, it may not always be possible to do the proper correction immediately. In this case, always keep safety in mind—often this means that you should just wait for another opportunity when you do have the space and circumstances to do the correction safely and effectively.

4.2 A–D **In this sequence of photos, you can see when the horse starts to have a bad attitude and pin his ears at me . . .**

. . . I immediately go back to groundwork and start moving his feet. After a few minutes of my Lungeing for Respect—Stage Two exercise, with enough changes of direction to really get his feet moving, the horse is glad to stand still and accept the saddle with a "smile" on his face.

Horses challenge the pecking order every single day

If you put 10 horses from 10 different barns and 10 different owners in a 4-acre pasture all at once, there would be no pecking order. It would be somewhat disturbing to them, and they might bite and kick a little, but once you start to bring out the hay and grain, you'll see which horses are going to be dominant and which are going to be more passive. Over the next week, you'll see the pecking order emerge, Number 1 through Number 10, and every day these horses will challenge each other to try to move up in the order.

You and your horse are in a herd of two. As such, every day your horse will challenge you to see if you are still worthy to be his leader. A lot of people take this personally. Don't. It's just part of a horse's nature, just like a child's—to check to see if the rules you have set are still in place (photo 12.4).

Some horses will challenge you more than others. These aren't necessarily the bad horses. On the contrary, in fact these are most often the horses that, once they confirm you as their leader, will go above and beyond what other horses are willing to do for you.

Another factor to consider as your horse challenges you is what may still be in the back of his mind—what he thinks he could do—if he "wins." What has he been allowed to get away with in a previous experience? What behavior could he slide back to? You can retrain behavior, but the more "baggage" the horse has, the more difficult maintaining your retraining can be.

Just remember, mate, horses always know what you know, and they know what you don't know—and they're always going to check to see if you are still worthy of their respect. So when your horse challenges you, be very clear and consistent and *move his feet* to protect your place at the top of the pecking order in your little herd of two.

12.4 **Some horses will test the boundaries you set every single day. Getting a horse to sidepass away from you will encourage him to use the "thinking" side of his brain and so become more respectful toward you.**

Lesson 13

Horses are creatures of habit

Horses don't understand "right" or "wrong,"
they just know what they've been allowed to do.

HER 10-year-old gelding was about as disrespectful and pushy as a horse could be. When she started to work with the horse as I instructed on the first day of my clinic's groundwork exercises, he just refused to do anything. Instead, he continuously tried to bite, kick, and push into her.

After watching for a few minutes, I took the horse to one side and started working with him to give her an example to follow. Every time he tried to bite or kick me, I just made his feet move with my Lunging for Respect—Stage Two exercise, and lots of changes in direction—really making him hustle his feet.

She watched without a word, and then said, "I don't know why he acts this way."

"What do you do at home when he tries to bite you?" I asked, still working with the horse.

"I ignore it."

"What do you do when he tries to kick you?"

"I get away from him so he can't hurt me—and then I leave him alone."

"Does he pin his ears at you?"

"Well, yes, sometimes."

"What do you do?"

"I get out of his way." She looked a little sheepish at first, and then decided to try to explain. "I figure he'll stop it if I give him a little space and more love and attention."

"What you're doing is teaching him to behave this way with

Left: 13.1 **A horse's habit is like a groove on an old LP record. The longer a habit persists—good or bad—the deeper the groove gets.**

you," I said. "Every time he does something bad and you ignore it or leave him alone, you're telling him it's okay to be that way."

"So what do I do?"

"Every time he does something nasty," I said, "make his feet move—just like I'm doing right now. Pretty soon, he'll get the idea that if he's nice, he gets to stand there and relax. If he's nasty, he's going to be moving those feet and needing some air."

As I watched that woman learn to move her horse's feet in response to his dangerous and disrespectful behavior, I watched a transformation take place right before my eyes. By the end of that clinic, they both had a completely new picture of each other.

The lesson here is that the worst, most dangerous, most disrespectful horse in the world wasn't born that way. Just like the most terrible inmate on death row, he was born into this world with no opinions, no habits, and no perceptions. What happened in his world since that moment determined how he behaved.

That's why it makes such a difference to get to foals as soon as they're born to begin imprinting them and desensitizing them. The sooner you can get to a horse, the more you can curb bad behavior, and the sooner you get to an older horse, the better chance you have of rehabilitating him from whatever "baggage" he carries from earlier negative experiences.

Plant the right seed

Whatever a horse practices, he gets good at. If he practices biting, he gets good at biting. If he practices being respectful, he gets good at being respectful.

I have another little saying on this topic: "When a horse does something once, it plants a seed in his mind. When he does it again, it starts to grow as a habit. When he does it a third time, this behavior starts to mature into an ingrained habit." So, if it's good behavior, it's a good habit; if it's a bad behavior, it's a bad habit. The horse doesn't *know* if it's a good or bad habit. He just knows that he has been allowed to do it.

The most important thing to remember here is that regardless of what the horse does, good *or* bad, once he does it three times, the behavior is well on its way to becoming an ingrained habit (photo 13.2).

Think of an old LP record going around and around. Now imagine that the horse's mind is like the needle—just like old record players

13.2 **Getting a horse to run up to you in the pasture, eager to be caught, is a sign of his respect and a good relationship. A horse that runs from you and is hard to catch is showing you a lack of respect.**

13.3 **I flex my horse like this hundreds of times in the beginning stages of his training to make staying light, soft, and supple a habit for him.**

have—with a really sharp tip. But this needle never moves. It stays on that one part of the record, and every time it goes around, each revolution represents an action of the horse. In one revolution, the action starts the groove. With the second revolution, it's a habit. By that third revolution, you have a pretty deep groove, an ingrained habit. The more times it goes around, the more times the horse repeats this action, the deeper and deeper the groove gets. The deeper the groove gets, the more the horse's mind will always be drawn back to it (photo 13.3).

This is especially true with older horses. If a horse is 10 years old and a habit has been there all his life, that record could have gone around thousands and thousands of times. By now the habit has made a great big groove in the record.

When we have to retrain the horse and get him to form other, *better* habits, we've got to first get the needle to come out of its deep, well-established groove, and then set it down on another part of the record to start a new groove, or habit. Then, every time the needle goes around in the new place—in other words, every time we get the horse to repeat the new action, we start to deepen the new groove (photos 13.4 A & B).

The problem with the old groove, however, is that at first, gravity will keep pulling the needle, or the horse's mind, back toward it. In fact, when you first begin to work with and practice a new habit, it will be very

13.4 A & B **My horse is walking off as I try to get on. Letting your horse do this just makes this bad habit get worse.**

To correct this problem, I get off and redirect his energy backward with a lot of hustle. Every time you correct a horse, you start to build a new habit. Over time, and with enough practice, the new habit can become as ingrained as the old one!

13.5 A–C **Horses don't know right or wrong—they just know what they've been allowed to do. In this photo, my horse turns his rump toward me when I enter his pen, so in turn I create pressure by swinging the lead rope toward those hindquarters to make him feel uncomfortable.**

As soon as he turns and gives me two eyes, I immediately take away the pressure and reward him.

Remember: Two eyes are always better than two heels.

easy for the horse to slip back into his old habit, just as it is for the needle to slip back into its old groove.

The good news is that the more you practice the new habit and keep deepening the new groove, the harder and harder it will become for the needle to return to its old groove. Although the old groove will always be there, if this same horse lives to be 20, and you have practiced the "new" habit for 10 years, the grooves will then be equal. And eventually, once you've practiced the new habit longer than the old one, the new groove will be deeper.

The more consistent you are, and the more structured, the easier it is to set a new groove. But if you only work with a problem horse once a week or once every two weeks, it's going to be very difficult to get that horse out of that old groove. It can still be done, but it takes a lot more work.

So remember: Basically *everything* you do with your horse, good or bad, starts to create a groove. And, while you can retrain horses with bad habits, the longer a horse has had the habit, the harder it is to fix and the more disciplined and consistent you have to be.

When the record has a very small groove in it—that is, if the horse has a habit that has not persisted for very long—it won't take much effort at all to get him going in a new direction (photos 13.5 A–C).

Lesson 14

You have to allow a horse to make a mistake—and *then* correct it

Correcting a mistake after it occurs accelerates a horse's learning, while preventing a mistake just guarantees he will keep making it.

I TROT *my horse out along the side of the arena to begin the Follow the Fence exercise. This is the first day of this for this horse, so it's what I call the "concept lesson." I just want to give the horse a general idea of what I'm asking him to do.*

First, I visualize an imaginary line running parallel to the fence about 15 feet from it. If my horse stays at a trot in between the fence and that imaginary line, I leave him alone, and I consider this lesson a success.

But the second he crosses that imaginary line, I will slide my hand halfway down the rein closest to the fence and tip his nose back in toward the fence to move him back within the 15-foot zone I have established. I do this for about 10 to 15 minutes one direction, and then I turn and do the same thing in the other direction.

Tomorrow I may cut that imaginary area down to 10 feet wide, the next day to 4 feet, and by the end of the week I should be able to reach out and touch the fence as my horse stays at the gait I put him in and never leaves the fence. The reason I know this is how it will go is because I have made this horse responsible for his own feet by allowing him room to make mistakes and then learn from them.

I can't tell you how many people have trouble with this exercise. Why? Because most people tend to micromanage their horse's behavior—

Left:14.1 **Too many people micromanage their horses, never allowing them to make a mistake. For a horse to learn what you want, you have to allow him to first make a mistake and then correct it. In this picture, notice how my rein is loose and my horse is keeping himself in a straight line parallel to the fence.**

14.2 A & B **A great way to teach your horse to be responsible for his own feet is my Follow the Fence exercise. When you first try this exercise and put your horse on a loose rein, he will probably make the mistake of veering away from the fence. Let him commit completely to this mistake as I am here, then ...**

...steer him back toward the fence where you want him to be, and drop the rein to reward him. This is how you show him it is his responsibility to stay next to the fence.

and the *Follow the Fence* exercise really brings this out. The object here is to make your horse responsible for his own feet. So if you start pulling him back to the fence before he really commits to crossing that imaginary line—in effect, "babysitting" him—he'll never know how to "follow the fence" on his own.

Why is this exercise so important? If you don't let your horse make the mistake *before* you correct it, how will he ever even know it was a mistake? If you can use this exercise to understand the lesson about allowing your horse to make mistakes and then learn from them, you have reached a major milestone in his training—and yours (photos 14.2 A & B).

It's the same with the *Cruising* lesson at a canter. I see so many people, especially those with slower, lazier horses, start squeezing or kicking their horse the minute he starts to slow down. All the horse learns when this happens is that this rider will always "babysit" him to make him stay in the correct gait.

Instead, I tell people to make their horse responsible for his own feet and for maintaining the gait they've asked for—until they ask him to do something else. Let him break all the way down to a trot—and go ahead and allow him trot for a few steps—*before* you squeeze, cluck, and spank, if necessary, to get him back into the canter.

If he tends to speed up and get too fast, let him stay at that faster gait for a few steps, and *then* slow him down to remind him what he's supposed to be doing. The more you do this, the more your horse will understand his own role and responsibility—and the less you will have to micromanage his feet (photo 14.3).

Another area where I see a lot of people "babysitting" their horses is in my *Yielding the Forequarters* exercise. Instead of yielding and pivoting around the outside back foot, the horse just wants to walk forward in a circle, and they keep trying to stop him from moving forward by pulling back on the lead rope. What they need to do instead is *let* him walk forward, and *then* back him up about 10 steps and try again as if nothing happened. If you don't let the horse *commit* to the mistake of moving forward instead of yielding and pivoting, how is he ever going to realize that his choice of walking forward is a mistake at all?

Any time your horse is acting sour because there is somewhere in particular that he would rather be, such as the gate, the barn, or with his buddies, instead of spending all your time and energy trying to keep him away from those things, let him go there. And then move his feet. Hustle, hustle, hustle—back and forth and around and around—right near whatever "magnet" is drawing him. Then, once he starts to huff and puff a little bit, guide him away from that place to a spot he normally doesn't want to be and let him rest. After you repeat this a few times he will start to associate the place he thought he wanted to be with work and the place he didn't like with rest (photos 14.4 A–C).

14.3 **You teach a horse to be responsible for his own feet—and to maintain the direction and gait you've requested until you ask him to do something else—by riding a lot of steady miles as I am here. Remember: Ask for what you want, then allow him to learn by waiting for him to commit to a mistake, and THEN correct him.**

14.4 A–C **My horse likes to be with his buddies...**

...but I discourage this by making his feet hustle whenever he gets near them.

Then, after a few minutes, I take him off by himself to rest. It doesn't take long for a horse to realize that it's far easier to be off by himself than it is to be with his friends where he has to hustle and work.

Correct mistakes by making the right thing easy and the wrong thing difficult—and always rewarding the slightest try

One time a lady walked up to me in a clinic with an unusual trailering problem. Although her horse would load onto the trailer perfectly, as soon as his feet stopped, if you didn't fasten the lead rope within one second, he'd race backward flat out of the trailer, sometimes so fast he'd trip, flip over backward, or come out sideways. This had become so dangerous that she had to back everyone up 100 feet whenever she wanted to load or unload her horse.

This woman had tried everything in the world to solve this problem, from giving him treats, to making him stay in the trailer longer, to punishing him, to pulling on the lead rope. The last thing she had tried was suggested to her by some old cowboy. He told her to back the trailer several feet into a lake so that when the horse raced out backward, he'd fall into the water and scare himself, and so not try to race out quickly anymore.

This plan had indeed worked. The horse was so afraid to back out of the trailer that he wouldn't even get back in it for six months. This "solution" had only succeeded in making the horse associate his fear with the trailer.

So, using the principle of letting the horse commit to the mistake and then making the right thing easy and the wrong thing difficult, here's how I fixed this problem. I led the horse into the trailer and he just walked straight in. As soon as I got to the front of the trailer he stopped, panicked, and ran back. As he ran backward, I just let the rope slide through my hands, and I ran with him. And as soon as we got out of the trailer, I lunged him using my *Lungeing for Respect—Stage One and Two* exercises. Hustle, hustle, hustle. Stop, turn, stop, turn, hustle, hustle, hustle!

I did this for five minutes or so, then turned and walked him back into the trailer. Again, he got to the front and as soon as his feet stopped he raced backward. And again, I went with him. The second he got all four feet outside the trailer, I began lungeing him. I made him run and hustle for about five minutes, and then I took him back into the trailer. By taking the pressure off when he got inside the trailer, I gave him a chance to associate being in the trailer with the opportunity to rest (photos 14.5 A–D).

For about the first five times he went back into the trailer, the minute his feet stopped moving he ran backward. By then I had been working him for a good 25 minutes, and he was starting to huff and puff a little

14.5 A–D **This horse is trying to run back out of the trailer very quickly.**

The more you try to slow his speed down by holding onto the lead rope, the more trapped and claustrophobic he feels.

Making the horse work outside the trailer by moving his feet causes him to look for a better place to be, which is inside the trailer.

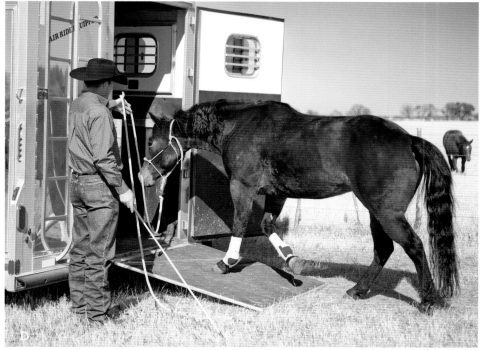

So basically, it comes down to work outside the trailer, and rest inside the trailer. Once this horse understood that, he stopped being in such a rush to get out.

bit. So on that sixth time when he got up to the front of the trailer, he stopped and stood there for about five seconds before he bolted backward. I kept repeating the same procedure, but each time after that he'd stay 10 to 20 seconds longer before he'd race back out.

After about 10 more times I could get him to stand still in the trailer on a loose rope for five or six minutes before he started moving backward. By this time, he was really tired and sweaty and looking for a place to rest. That's half the secret. I had showed him that the place to rest was *in* the trailer.

Once I could get him to stand there five or six minutes, I started trying to back him slowly out of the trailer. As soon as I started to back him, however, he raced backward again. So I repeated the same lungeing exercise. Then I led him into the trailer and let him rest. Five minutes later, I backed him out again. The first three or four times I did this he still backed out as fast as he could. But on about the fifth time, he started to just creep backward. He wasn't in any hurry to get outside, because he knew being outside the trailer meant I was going to make him work again.

It took me about an hour and a half to get him to back out of the trailer like a snail. He had figured out that inside the trailer meant rest and relaxation and outside the trailer meant work. On the next day of the clinic we brought him out again, but before I loaded him the first time, I did a little preparation. I lunged him for about five minutes at the end of the trailer before I put him inside. When I put him on the trailer to let him rest, he didn't move a muscle. I stayed there beside him for 10 minutes and then I backed him off. He just crept out ever so slowly, because he was like, "Hey, let's not get out of the trailer so fast, Clinton; in fact, let's just stay here in the trailer. It's the best place to be."

This horse was a tough case, but a great example of allowing the horse to make the mistake, consistently correcting the mistake, and then letting him find the right answer on his own. It's more about making the wrong thing difficult and the right thing easy to turn my idea into his idea.

Don't pull back

Another key concept here is that most people would try to *stop* the horse from backing off quickly by pulling back on the lead rope. Have you ever noticed that the more you want to try to stop a horse from backing the faster he wants to go? You pull back on the lead rope, the horse raises his head and hits the top of the trailer, gets more frightened, and moves back even faster. The more you say, "Don't back out fast!" the faster he wants to back out.

However, if instead you say, "Hey, back off fast, it's fine with me!" and then make him hustle, hustle, hustle when he gets out of the trailer, after a few times the horse will be quite content to stay on that trailer and be in no hurry at all to back out of it.

Let the mistake happen

If you see a man outside a bank with a gun, can the police arrest him for bank robbery? Of course not! What you have to do is allow him to enter the bank, commit to the robbery, and *then* arrest him. Just like that bank robber, mate, you've got to let your horse commit to his mistake and then catch him red-handed to make the lesson stick.

Lesson 15

Treat abused horses, rescue horses, and other "special cases" the same as any other horse

Making excuses and special allowances for an abused horse's bad behavior will only limit him; treating him the same as any other horse will accelerate his progress.

"CLINTON,

I just wanted to come find you and talk about my horse." The demeanor of the petite woman standing in front of me was timid, almost apologetic, and her overall manner was very soft-spoken.

It was the start of a clinic. I didn't know which horse was hers, but I could have guessed what she was going to say even before she said it. I had not been doing clinics for very long in the United States, but already I was familiar with this request. In fact, it happened all the time.

Sure enough, she said, "I just want to spend a little bit of one-on-one time with you before we get started." She shifted uncomfortably and glanced back at the group of horses behind her. "You see, my horse has been abused. And because she's been abused, she gets very upset about certain things." She stood there, waiting for my reaction.

I nodded.

"Because my horse has been abused, she has these little fits from time to time, and I just want to let you know about this so you'll understand what's going on with her. And I just wanted to let you know why she's probably not going to be able to do what all the other horses can do, because they haven't been abused. She's probably going to need some special adjustments to these exercises—and you may even want to change what we do at this clinic a little bit to allow for her needs."

Left:15.1 **People often make excuses for why their horse doesn't behave, and one is they mistakenly believe that previously abused horses need special allowances. This woman is explaining her horse's terrible past and asking what modifications she should make because of the horse's trust issues.**

I looked at this tiny lady and said, "You know what? That's terrible. I'm so sorry that your horse was abused." I looked in the direction of the horses, then back at the lady. "Um, is your horse being abused any more?"

Her eyes widened with shock, "Oh no, heavens no!" she said. "I would never hurt my horse!"

I smiled and said, "Right. Well then, today's a good day, because your horse is no longer being abused." I paused for a moment, glanced at her nametag, and said, "I'll tell you what I want you to do, Emily."

She moved a step closer, so as not to miss a word of the special instructions I was about to give her.

"I want you to act like you just bought this horse from me this morning," I said. "You don't know where she came from, you don't know how old she is, and don't know how much she's been ridden. You have zero history on this horse at all."

She took a step back. Her shock had now turned into confusion. "Why?"

"Emily," I said, "what you're doing is you're carrying around all these big bags of excuses for why your horse acts the way she does—and as long as you keep carrying around these big bags of excuses, your horse is never going to get any better.

"If this horse was abused by human beings," I continued, "and the horse was starved and beaten every day for a year, and we took her out of that environment and put her in a brand new pasture across the road with 10 new horses—horses she had never met before—would those horses treat your horse any differently? Would they say, 'Okay, everybody, listen up! Nobody eats until this new horse has had all she wants—just look at how skinny this poor little thing is. No, No, NO! She gets the shelter—she's been homeless! Stop it! Everybody leave this horse alone! She just needs love. She needs caring. She needs cherishing." I looked at Emily, who was laughing by now. "Would the other horses do that?"

"Well, no, I guess they wouldn't," she said.

"Right!" I said, "Those 10 other horses would not treat your horse any differently whatsoever. They'd still kick her, they'd still bite her, and they'd still chase her around. And then again, she might chase them around! She might even be number one in their pecking order!

"My point is, Emily, those horses are not going to treat your *horse any differently whether she's been abused by humans or not. So if horses don't treat each other any differently when one of them has been abused, why should we treat them any differently?"*

I could tell this was making sense to Emily, so I said, "What I want you to do in this clinic is pretend that you just bought this horse from me today. Let's say that I don't know anything about the horse because I won her last night in a poker game, and I was drunk and can't remember any of the details. So this morning, Emily, I'm cashing in. I need some cash for this horse and you just bought her from me. Here's your horse." I pretended to hand her an imaginary lead rope.

"Okay," Emily said. "But what do I do when she acts up?"

"If you just go out there today in the clinic, and every time you want to make an excuse for why your horse is misbehaving, you remember that you don't know why she's misbehaving, be- cause you don't know anything about her, you'll be amazed at what will get done."

I watched Emily's amazement grow over the next three days as her horse quickly responded and soon began to behave just like all the other horses.

This lesson first presented itself years ago. Back then it happened a lot, but now that I've built more credibility in the United States and peo- ple know they can trust me and just follow my Method, it doesn't happen quite so much. The frequency of this situation in the beginning, however, did show me the consistency of its result.

When people begin to treat an abused or rescue horse just like any other horse, it is absolutely amazing to see how quickly the horse comes around and starts *acting* like every other horse (photos 15.2 A–C). He just turns into a regular old broke, respectful horse. And, almost without exception, this change comes about very, very quickly.

On the other hand, the more people protect these horses, the sil- lier and sillier they get. I know it doesn't make sense, but with horses the more you *try* to scare them—the more you try to make them flip out— the less they want to overreact and the quieter they will get.

Now of course it would be different if you were physically hurting the horse—if you were hitting him or kicking him or whipping him. And in the previous story about the trailer in the lake (see Lesson 14, p. 111), even though they were *trying* to scare the horse, all right, the horse didn't get quieter because he found a way to relieve himself of the pressure by run-

15.2 A–C When you treat an abused or rescue horse just like any other horse, it is absolutely amazing to see how quickly he will start behaving like any other horse. My work with this rescue horse named Cider in my RFD-TV series actively demonstrates that although abuse is a terrible thing, once a horse is brought back to health, treating him just the same as you would treat any other horse breaks the cycle of abuse-related behavior.

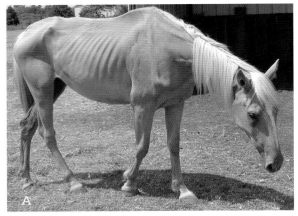

15.3 **Horses don't treat other horses differently if they've been abused by a human in the past, so why should we?**

15.4 **All horses—including abused or "special cases"— benefit from spending time at the "Tree and Post of Knowledge." Tie your horse and let him stand for a while after you work with him. It will greatly increase his ability to retain what he has learned.**

ning away. The only way a horse gets quieter is if you can keep the pressure on him until he relaxes and realizes it is not going to hurt him.

How "scary" can be good

What I'm talking about here is trying to frighten the horse with things that are never going to hurt him—noises, plastic bags, a rope thrown at him—and desensitizing him by slapping the Handy Stick and String on the ground. We're doing things that he *thinks* might hurt him, but in reality will never, ever hurt him.

Just as other horses will in the pasture, we're going to do what we need to do with our rescue horse to establish the same rules, set the same boundaries, instill the same behaviors, and maintain the same pecking order (photo 15.3).

So remember that whether you buy a horse that's been abused, or an abused or rescue horse is given to you, you have to try to treat him it no differently than any other horse. Sure, these horses may require that you do more of one particular exercise or another. They may require more desensitizing or sensitizing. Some exercises may take a little longer to master, and you may have to spend more time in one category. But isn't that the same with all horses?

If you don't treat an abused or rescue horse any differently than you would any other horse, you'll most likely discover progress that will amaze you, just as it did Emily (photo 15.4).

Lesson 16

The more times you pick yourself up off the ground, the better your "groundwork" gets

Why horses buck — and how preparing a horse to be ridden from the ground is the key to staying safer in the saddle.

WITHOUT

any real warning, I felt the unmistakable hump rising up through the colt's back, and before I could react, I was flying through the air and landing in the dirt. As one of Gordon McKinlay's young apprentices, I was still learning.

Luckily, I landed well and the only thing hurt was my pride. Usually, I was more thorough with my groundwork. Usually, I did a better job of preparing the horse to be ridden. But today I had been in a hurry and had cut a few corners; I had hurried things along a little too much. And now one of Gordon's favorite sayings echoed in my head: "The more times you pick yourself up off the ground, the better your 'groundwork' gets."

As I spat the dirt out of my mouth on that day long ago in Australia, I learned a lesson about bucking horses I have never forgotten—and since then it has proved itself to be true more times than I can count. This lesson actually has two parts, and both of them deal with the issue of bucking.

First, hurrying through my groundwork and not doing *enough* of the right type of exercises on the ground had caused the horse to use the reactive side of his brain and buck me off. And second, I was still way too slow at my *One-Rein Stops*.

Gordon had told me that if you can bend the horse's head around and do a *One-Rein Stop* the minute the horse even thinks about bucking,

Left: 16.1 **When a horse kicks up and crow hops as seen here, it is merely a sign of his lack of respect for you and his reluctance to move his feet.**

you can usually stop him. But timing is critical on this, and to recognize the signs that a horse is about to buck and to bend his head around fast enough takes practice.

Clearly, I had not yet practiced this enough. By the time I had thought, "Oh my goodness! I need to bend his head around!" it was too late. So that day I realized the truth in another of Gordon's favorite sayings: "The more times you spit dirt out of your mouth, the quicker your *One-Rein Stops* get."

In Australia, I used to be a professional horse trainer. Now I'm a professional people trainer, but it all started with training the horses. People used to bring me all kinds of problem horses—horses that would rear, buck, and bolt. If someone sent me a horse that had a bad habit of bucking people off, the last thing I'd do is get straight on that horse and ride him the first day.

Instead, I would first *prepare* the horse to be ridden by working with him for five to seven days on the ground, getting him soft and supple and using the thinking side of his brain. Then, when I did start riding him, about 99.9 percent of the time he didn't even *think* about bucking. You see, I got rid of all that bad stuff on the ground so when I got on him, I was safe. If I had tried to ride the horse the first day, I guarantee you he would have tried to buck me off. The key is preparing the horse. Remember: "The more times you pick yourself up off the ground, the better your 'groundwork' gets."

Preventing the bucking habit

When I was an apprentice for Gordon and we broke in two-year-olds, there were a lot of other guys in the apprenticeship who didn't care if their horse bucked a little bit; in fact, they kind of *liked* it when their horse bucked. They'd fan the horse with their hat, make noise, and put on a bit of a show for the girls. I on the other hand, hated it.

I never liked riding bucking horses because I didn't like the chance of getting hurt so I couldn't ride. As a result, any time a horse really bucked I didn't stay on. I wasn't very good at riding bucking horses because I didn't practice it very much. However, although some of those other guys could *really* ride a bucking horse well, what I also noticed was that when they sent their horses back to the owners, a lot of these owners—our customers—were really unhappy with the job they did. Many of these horses bucked their owners off as soon as they got home.

The horses I trained, on the other hand, rarely ever bucked anybody off after they went home. Why was that? Because I never let my horses learn the habit of bucking. I just never let them think that bucking was something acceptable to do.

Debunking old cowboy logic

You have probably heard the old theory, "When you get bucked off, you have to just get right back up on that bronc and show him who's boss!" I don't believe in that. Whenever I get bucked off a colt, the *last* thing I would ever do is get straight back on. If you get right back on, chances are he's just going to buck you off again. It's just that simple. I want to figure out why he's bucking. Usually, the answer is because I've done a poor job of preparation on the ground.

So, as long as I'm not injured, here's what I do instead. I immediately take hold of the lead rope and start moving the horse's feet—forward, backward, left, and right.

Then I do my *Lunging for Respect—Stage Two* exercise, back him up, and sidepass him down a fence line. I repeat this sequence over and over again. I really hustle his feet until he is very tired and sweaty and using the thinking side of his brain.

Then I'll get back on him and ride him. A lot! I'm going to keep hustling his feet from the saddle until I make him regret bucking me off. I'm going to bring him back dripping with sweat, and I'm going to tie him up for three or four hours, and then I'm going to go ride him again. (Note: In a cold climate, be sure to apply a cooler before tying the horse, and make sure to monitor him.) Tying a horse up after you've worked him hard does two things. It gives him a chance to "get his air back," and it gives him a chance to process the the work you just did. This is not punishment—it is allowing him time to absorb the lesson. The very worst thing you can do after working with your horse on a particular issue is to put him in his stall and feed him. Once he gets his mind on eating, you can be pretty sure it's no longer on you!

Now, if I am injured when I get bucked off a horse, I may have to just put the horse away. That's never an ideal situation, because then the horse realizes that bucking you off got a release of pressure; however, sometimes you have to do what you have to do. But the next time I get that horse out, I may not ride him right away. I may just do groundwork for three or four days to prepare him to be ridden again.

16.2 A–C If your horse is giving you trouble and threatening to buck on the trail, don't be afraid to get off and do some groundwork right then and there. Remember, it's far better to get off and get control from the ground than to stay on and get thrown off.

Here I'm doing Lungeing for Respect—Stage Two with lots of changes of direction...

D

...and then the Sending exercise between trees.

Once you get your horse calm and using the "thinking" side of his brain, as my horse is here, just get back on and continue your ride.

Another thing to note here is that if a horse starts to buck and I do get him stopped by bending his head and neck around and doing a *One-Rein Stop* rather than getting thrown, I'll usually then get off and immediately start moving his feet from the ground.

It's crucial that when you get off you *immediately* get the horse moving. Don't get off and put him up, or get off and let him rest. If you do either of those things, you're teaching him that bucking is what got you to get off his back. Hustle his feet so that he understands that bucking was a *big* mistake (photos 16.2 A–D).

Get it right from the beginning

The first time I saddle a colt, he can buck as hard as he wants to while I'm on the ground. But from the second time on, I never, ever, let a horse buck—even without a rider. Not even when he's just loose in the round pen, or with just a halter, lead rope, and a saddle. I never let a horse develop the habit of wanting to buck with the saddle on. Period.

After that second saddling, every time a horse starts to buck with the saddle on, I'll give him something else to think about. I'll back him up, change directions, and redirect his feet (photos 16.3 A & B). Horses are creatures of habit, so if you let a horse get into the habit of bucking, that's what he'll always do.

I remember Gordon and some of the other apprentices would always get mad at me because we'd be about to go mustering cattle and plan to leave around 6:30 A.M., and it would be time to load our horses up on the big cattle truck. I was always the last one to load my horse on the truck, because I'd be out there till the very last second doing ground-work—wiggling my rope, using the bag and flag, lungeing, sidepassing, and flexing my horse.

I always got up extra early—before anyone else—so I would have more time to do enough groundwork to make sure that my two-year-old wasn't going to buck me off. They'd be yelling at me, "C'mon Clinton! Hurry up!" However, even though everyone got frustrated with me for holding things up a little bit, I very rarely got in a wreck when we were mustering.

When you're first learning my method, groundwork *does* take a lot of time. But with practice, you do get a lot faster, and eventually you learn how to be thorough and efficient in all your groundwork. For example, when I was first starting out, when I'd get a wild brumby it might take me three hours to get him caught and gentle enough so I could do some groundwork with him, bend and flex him, and get a saddle on his back. Now I can complete that same process in about an hour.

Even though Gordon sometimes got frustrated with me because I spent so much time on my groundwork, he also realized that being slow and doing it right was a lot better than being fast and doing it wrong. So he did cut me a little slack on that. And one thing he would never make me do was get on a horse that wasn't ready to be ridden.

I actually pride myself on *not* being able to ride a bucking horse. Ever since my apprenticeship with Gordon, I have come to understand that because I never learned to like riding bucking horses, I have had

16.3 A & B **The better your preparation on the ground before you get on, the better your chance of having a safe and successful ride. Remember: Groundwork equals respect, which leads to control that helps ensure safety. Here I'm doing Stirrup Driving and Sending with this colt before getting on.**

16.4 A–C **The way Gordon McKinlay taught me to start colts was the safest method I've ever seen for breaking in horses. For the first few rides, we'd work the horse as a team—one person on the ground, directing the horse's feet, and one in the saddle.**

Here professional clinician Shana Terry is first flexing this colt on both sides...

...and then I drive him from the ground while she rides as a "passenger" in the saddle.

A

very few horses actually buck me off. The key to learning this lesson for me was continuing to do an extremely good job of preparing the horse to be ridden.

Is the horse ready to be ridden?

When I'd break in a horse for Gordon, he'd walk up to me and ask, "Clinton, is this horse ready to ride?" If I said, "No Gordon, he's not quite ready," Gordon would just say, "Okay then, I'll just come back in a couple of days and check on you." Then he'd come back in a couple of days and ask the same question. If at that time I said, "Yes, Gordon, he's ready to ride," we'd ride the horse.

The way Gordon taught me to start colts was the absolute safest method I've ever seen to break in horses. For the first few rides, we always rode the horse as a team. The way this works is in the round pen: I'd ride the horse and Gordon would be on the ground directing the horse's feet. I've seen a lot of colt-starting methods since then, and I can tell you with absolute certainty that Gordon's approach is the very safest way to start two-year-olds (photos 16.4 A–C).

Does your horse buck?

First, let's define what bucking really is. What a lot of people call bucking is when the horse's front legs stay on the ground and he kicks up his back legs. That's not bucking. Bucking to me is what you see at the rodeo: All four feet are off the ground, the horse's head is down low, his mouth is open, and he is bellowing like a cow giving birth. The horse is 40 feet in the air, and the other thing that will tip you off that this is true bucking is that *you'll* be *48* feet in the air. In other words, when a horse is *really* bucking, you know it (photo 16.5).

The kicking up, "crow-hopping," or as we call it in Australia, "pig-rooting" (I have no idea why it's called this), are simple demonstrations of the horse's lack of respect. What type of horse usually kicks up? A fat, lazy horse; a horse that doesn't want to go forward. When you ask this horse to go from a trot to a canter, and he kicks up with his back legs, it's his way of telling you to get lost. Most hot, nervous horses don't kick up that much because they *want* to go forward—so much so that this becomes another kind of problem.

On the other hand, most horses that are *really* bucking are not showing a lack of respect. They are most likely reacting to fear: fear of you being on his back, you being in the saddle, the girth, the flank girth, your legs, the spurs, or something that jumped out of the bushes in front of him. Something has caused him to use the reactive side of his brain. That's how most horses learn to buck.

And sometimes, once a horse has dumped a rider three or four times and has gotten into the habit of bucking, I think a horse starts bucking out of a lack of respect and out of habit—not so much out of fear. At this point, what may have started out as a fear issue has now turned into a lack-of-respect issue.

Here's the remedy

The good news is that regardless of whether your horse is kicking up or crow-hopping to demonstrate his lack of respect—or truly bucking out of fear or habit—there are several ways to fix the problem.

If a horse wants to kick up, which means he has a lack of respect and doesn't want to go forward, go back and get his feet moving better on the ground. Put him in a round pen, and then point, cluck, and spank—first spank the ground, and if necessary, spank him—until you get him cantering around that round pen.

16.5 **What a lot of people call "bucking" is when the horse's front legs stay on the ground and he kicks up his back legs (see p. 122). That's not bucking. When a horse is really bucking, you know it! This is the best example I know of a horse that's really bucking, an old print of a famous Australian bucking horse named Curio. I have this print hanging on my office wall to remind me what a true bucking horse looks like!**

16.6 **When you squeeze and cluck to ask your horse to move and he kicks up, spank him side to side with your mecate as I am here. If he kicks up again, spank him again!**

Get him so hooked onto you that as soon as you point and cluck he starts loping straightaway. Get his feet really hustling on a lunge line, as well. If you get rid of that laziness and lack of respect on the ground first, then when you get on him, he'll be a lot more willing to go forward.

Then, when you *do* get on the horse, first squeeze with both legs to ask him to go forward. Wait for a count of two, and if he doesn't go, cluck. Wait for another count of two, and when he doesn't go forward, spank him side to side with the end of your mecate. If you spank with rhythm and he kicks up with both his back legs, what do you do? You spank him again: whack, whack (photo 16.6).

Often, when you do spank like this, he just kicks up again. So now what do you do? You spank him again: whack, whack. You have to keep repeating this until at some point, the horse realizes that every time his back legs leave the ground, you are going to make his butt ache— and every time he keeps his feet on the ground, you'll leave him alone.

One thing I want to be clear about here is that you have to be a confident enough rider to go through this process. If you're not, and you make sure you do your groundwork thoroughly and correctly, you probably won't even have any more of that kicking up under saddle. Your horse will more than likely go forward as soon as you squeeze and cluck. Or with a little bit of a spank, he'll go forward.

If you've done a poor job on the ground—or if you've quit too soon— then you've got to fix it under saddle. To me, that's not that big of a deal, but if you are not that good of a rider, or if you're inexperienced or fearful, this might be too much for your ability. So if that's the case, just be sure you do a better job on the ground, and then maybe have a more experienced rider ride the horse for a few days and get his feet moving.

It's also important to note that if I've got a horse that's not just kicking up or crow-hopping, but is actually *bucking* like he's in a rodeo, the *last* thing I want to do is spank him. That's why you have to understand the difference. If you spank a horse that is truly bucking, he'll only buck harder.

What I'll do with that particular horse is try to do a *One-Rein Stop*—bend his head and neck around to one side and try to get him to disengage his hindquarters—to get his hind legs to cross. By bending his head and neck and *Disengaging the Hindquarters*, you take away his ability to rear and buck because his hind legs are moving laterally (photo 16.7). As soon as he's stopped, I'll get off him and go right to work moving his feet from the ground.

16.7 **Never spank a horse that is truly bucking as in photo 16.5; he'll only buck harder. Instead, pull his head around in a One-Rein Stop, and then do my Yielding the Hindquarters from a Standstill exercise as I'm doing here. This gets his hind legs to cross, and the lateral movement takes away his ability to buck. Once you get him stopped and his hindquarters disengaged, get off and go right to work moving his feet from the ground.**

It has been said that a wise man learns from his mistakes—and a wiser man learns from the mistakes of others. For a lot of people, especially when you're young, you have to feel the pain of your own mistakes before a lesson can really sink in. I don't know why this is—maybe because when you're young, many times you're also stupid. But when it comes to bucking horses, mate, be the wiser by learning from *my* mistakes and spare yourself the pain of learning it firsthand.

Lesson 17

Consistency is your greatest ally— and inconsistency your greatest enemy

Consistent practice in even small increments of time will build stronger mental and physical habits with your horses — and yield big-time results.

MAY 2009

Sunday	Monday	Tuesday	Wednesday	Thursday	Friday	Saturday
					1	2
3	4	5	6	7	8	9
10	11	12	13	14	15	16
17	18	19	20	21	22	23
24 / 31	25	26	27	28	29	30

WHEN she showed up each week for her lesson, this lady I was teaching to ride (when I was back in Australia) always started by complaining about her lack of progress. And she was right. The simple truth was that she wasn't getting better—and neither was her horse. The worst part was she was kind of blaming me for it.

I said, "Are you riding the horse on the days between our lessons?"

"Well, no, I don't have a lot of time," she said. "I only work with him when you're here."

"There's your problem right there!" I said.

She looked confused.

"I'm not a miracle worker," I said. "I'm giving you the information each week, but I can't make your horse go train himself in the pasture. If you're really unhappy about your lack of progress, you're going to have to make the effort to find the time to work with your horse between lessons."

I could tell she didn't really believe me, so I proposed an experiment. I said, "Why don't you practice what I show you in this lesson every day for the next week, and when we have our next lesson, let's see if we can tell any difference."

Reluctantly, she agreed.

The next week when she came for her lesson, she was beaming. "I did it!" she said. "I practiced what you showed me last week every single day—and guess what? You were right!"

Left:17.1 **Remember: Consistency is your greatest ally and inconsistency your greatest enemy. The more consistent you are with your horse, the better and faster you will get results.**

I just smiled and for the next hour enjoyed watching the amazing transformation she had brought about in her horse—and in her own riding—with just one week of consistent practice.

This lesson illustrates one of the biggest problems I see with people training their horses. With jobs, families, and busy lives, it is hard for people to even imagine that they could find the time to train their horse every day. But here's the secret: It's not the *amount* of time you spend with your horse every day, but rather the *consistency* of actually spending time working with him every day, that counts.

Why do you send kids to school five days a week? Children learn from repetition. Every time they learn new information through consistent repetition, they can build on that learning with more new information. It takes a child roughly 13 years to graduate from high school. That's going to school five days a week, kindergarten through twelfth grade.

But what if they were only to go to school *two* days a week? Would they still be able to graduate? Of course they would. It would just take a lot longer. Even though they would still get the same information in each lesson, their retention value wouldn't be very high because of the time lapse between lessons.

It's the same with learning any new skill, such as when I learn to tie a new knot. When a person teaches me a new knot, I tie it in front of him two or three times, then I repeat the process as many times as I can with him watching me until I can remember how to tie that knot without him standing there. If he just shows me how to tie it and then I tie it a couple of times and send him on his way, I'll probably forget it by the next day. When I first learn something, I need to do it over and over again to form a connection, or a habit, between my mind and my hands of how to tie that knot (photo 17.2).

Training the mind *and* the body

It's much the same when you train a horse. He, too, is learning both mental and physical habits. In addition to training his mind to remember the new habit, every day a horse's body is adjusting to its new physical workload.

Think about when you first start working out your abs. You may not be able to do much on that first day, but after two weeks of steady, daily work, you will be able to do a lot more than you could that first

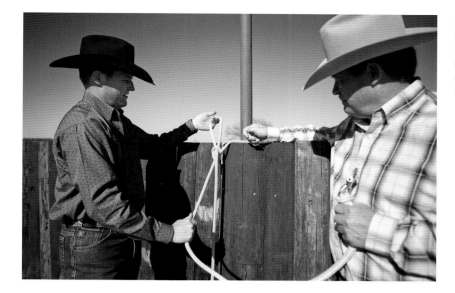

day because you have built on your progress each day, physically conditioning your muscles through consistent repetition. You didn't make this progress by doing four hours of abs training once a week, but by training your muscles for eight minutes every single day.

Find remarkable progress in tiny daily steps

If I had the choice between training a horse for 15 minutes—no more and no less—every single day, seven days a week, or training a horse for three hours once a week, assuming I was the only one working with the horse, I'd always take the 15 minutes a day (photo 17.3).

That's because even though I'm only working with him 15 minutes a day, each day I get to build on my progress. If on Monday I made a little bit of improvement, then on Tuesday I get to build on Monday's progress. On Wednesday I can build on Tuesday's progress, and so on.

But if I only work with my horse for three hours on Wednesday, even though it seems like I could get a lot more done because I have three hours, a horse can only physically and mentally take so much training at once. A horse will either run out of air or run out of mental capacity, and once he gets exhausted, it's hard for him to learn anything, because his focus has shifted to trying to rest.

The other trouble with working with a horse for three hours, one day a week, is if I don't work with him again for an entire week, I'll have to spend most of my three hours next week going back over what I

17.3 **If you have a choice between working with your horse 15 minutes a day several days a week, or three hours once a week, you'll make a lot more progress taking that 15 minutes a day.**

taught him this week. Each week I'll have to spend more and more time recapping what I did earlier, making it very difficult to ever introduce much new information.

In a perfect world, I like to train my horses six days a week with one day off. But even *I* don't often get to do that anymore because I'm traveling all over the country three or four days of every single week. So if you, too, can only work with your horse about three days a week, I'd recommend you do it three days in a row, rather than every other day. And, if you can only ride on the weekends, there's no harm in riding your horse twice a day.

Sometimes if I need to catch my horses up, I'll ride Saturday morning, Saturday evening, Sunday morning, and Sunday evening. That ends up being four rides—and the learning equivalent of riding them three or four days that week.

Dealing with "Mondayitis"

Here's what happens if you *don't* work with your horses on consecutive days. If I'm on tour for the weekend, and I come back on Monday to ride my horse, I always know that my horses are going to have what you might call "Mondayitis." They're off with the fairies, not paying attention, not listening, and so forth. So most of Monday's lesson is really not going to sink in much (photos 17.4 A & B).

17.4 A & B **The first day back after a break is what I call "Mondayitis," or the "throwaway lesson." On that day I'm only going to be able to reinforce what the horse already knows. It's important to let your horse blow off steam when you first bring him back from a break from work.**

After moving his feet for a while, you'll not only have rid him of his excess energy, but also reminded him to use the "thinking" side of his brain to calm himself down. Once my horse is calm, as my horse is here, I know he's ready to listen to me and make new progress.

In other words, most of Monday is going to be a refresher course. I'm not going to teach my horse anything new, but rather, my focus on Monday is going be reminding my horses of what they already know, saying, "Hey, do you remember how we did this and how we did that? Are you listening to me?"

I'll bet school teachers, especially those who teach little children, probably *hate* Mondays. It's got to be just chaotic. The kids aren't listening, they're talking about what they did over the weekend with their friends, they're doing show and tell, and they're just not mentally "hooked up" the way a teacher wants. But I'll also bet that by Thursday or Friday, those same kids are tuned into everything the teacher is saying and paying attention a whole lot better.

So if I work my horse on Monday and I get him listening and paying attention, but then I don't work with him again until Wednesday, by then he has come down with "Wednesdayitis," and I'm going to spend most of the lesson on Wednesday getting him to where he was when we quit on Monday. And then, if I don't work with him again until Friday, "Fridayitis" will strike, and the same thing is going to happen all over again.

So by giving my horse days off in between training sessions, I don't ever really get to build on anything. All I get to do is get the freshness out of my horse and get him mentally listening and prepared to learn. I call that first ride after time off a "throwaway ride," because although it's necessary, you can't really expect your horse to do that well.

On the other hand, if I work with my horse on Monday and get him listening, Tuesday's lesson will start exactly where Monday's left off, so I'll make a little bit of improvement on Tuesday. Wednesday's lesson should start where Tuesday's finished, and I'll make a little bit more improvement on Wednesday. So out of the three days I trained my horse this week, I actually got to make improvement on two of those days.

Understanding this is the key to avoiding frustration when you're trying to train your horse. Because I already know that when I come home from a tour or clinic and go to ride my horse that he's probably not going to be very good that first day, I don't get frustrated or disappointed. I just say to myself, "Today he's probably going to be fresh, looking around, and not hooked up the way I want him to be. But by the time I get finished, he'll be right on the money and tomorrow's lesson will be when I can make a lot of progress."

And if your job and family and responsibilities make it impossible to work with your horse for an hour and a half at a time, try doing 15 to 30 minutes every day and see what happens. If you don't have time to ride, try at least to do a little bit of groundwork. Do groundwork 15 minutes a day, three days a week, and then ride for 30 minutes three days a week.

Get creative about how you can be more consistent with maybe less time per training session. This approach will give you a lot more success with your horses.

Horses are nothing more than maintenance with legs

Horses never stay the same. If you want your horse to maintain a certain level of performance, you've got to be willing to put in a certain amount of time to help him do that. Just like a marathon runner has to run every day for a certain number of minutes at a certain intensity to maintain that level of fitness, horses—and especially younger and more inexperienced horses—need time and consistent training to maintain their level of performance.

The good news is that as a horse gets better trained or better broke, you won't have to keep spending as much time to keep him at the same level. For example, whereas my horses Mindy and Diez only have to be ridden two to three times a week to maintain their training and performance, my two-year-old needs much more than that. He needs consistent repetition to get good at what he's doing, so I need to put more time in there to help him maintain and build on his level of performance.

Just remember: For every one day you give your horse off, you're really giving him two days off—the day you think you're giving him off, and also the next time you work with him, or the "throwaway lesson." And even more important, it's not how long you spend with your horse, but the quality and consistency of the time you spend that makes the biggest difference.

So keep in mind that frequent little bits of consistent, focused training will get you a lot better results in the long run than bigger blocks of time that are inconsistent.

Lesson 18

Push the edges to enlarge your horse's comfort zone

Understanding the three zones of your horse's mind when it comes to fear will help you teach him to use the thinking side of his brain under pressure.

THE

woman gently lifted the very end of her lead rope up onto her horse's back and carefully slid it off. Then she picked up her Handy Stick and lightly swung it in a small circle, far away from her horse. It was easy to see the reason why she did this. Her horse was very flighty and jumpy, and it didn't take much at all to scare him.

I stood in the center of the arena and watched this woman just refuse to put any pressure on this horse. I had already told her several times over the course of the clinic that she was never going to get her horse to accept any desensitizing unless she really started to introduce it. Obviously, she was just kind of ignoring me and trying to hide in the corner of the clinic to avoid doing any of this to her horse. She was very protective of him, the type of person I had begun to recognize as the "There, there, Precious," kind of horse owner.

I decided to try again. I walked over to her and said, "Why do you not want to pressure your horse by using any of the desensitizing methods? Why do you never want to put enough pressure on him to get his feet to move?"

She looked a little sheepish and said, "Well, my horse is very scared and nervous and reactive, and I feel if I go and do all that stuff it's going to make him worse."

"Do you want your horse to learn how to deal with pressure?" I asked.

"Yes! Very much so!" she said. "I would like him to learn how to be calm even in a pressure situation."

Left:18.1 **A horse has what I call three zones in his mind: the "comfort zone," the "unsure zone," and the "life-threatening zone." Your horse will never learn how to handle pressure unless you put pressure on him. This horse is very unsure, but not yet in the "life-threatening zone." The key is to pressure him enough to get him into his unsure zone—and back—but not to "over-pressure" him to the point where he panics.**

"How do you think he is ever going to learn to be calm in a pressure situation if you never put him in a pressure situation?" I asked. "How would you ever learn to ride a bike if you never rode one?"

She shrugged, clearly perplexed.

"What you're doing is you're not pressuring your horse at all, so any time you even remotely pressure him, he comes undone."

She nodded vigorously.

"So here's what we're going to do," I said. "We're going to put your horse in a pressure situation, but we're not going to put him in such a high pressure situation that it will become dangerous for you or for your horse."

She had stopped nodding. I could see the panic and dread rising in her face.

"I don't want you to overcook your horse mentally or physically and send him into a 'life-threatening zone,'" I told her. "I only want you to apply just enough pressure that he has to somehow deal with it."

Her reluctance was clear. She said nothing, but I could tell she was hoping the ground would somehow swallow her up so she wouldn't have to do this.

"Now, in the beginning will he deal with this negatively?" I asked her. "Will he get frightened, get upset and want to run away? The answer is yes!"

She was nodding again.

"So what do you do?" I asked, and then answered my own question. "You maintain that pressure and wait for the horse to figure out what you want him to do, and when he does what you want, you take away the pressure."

"I'm just so afraid he'll get worse," she said, still doubtful.

"I have a little saying about this," I told her. "Sometimes things have to get worse before they can get better. You want to baby your horse and coax him into handling pressure, but the only way to really help him learn how to handle pressure is to just put him in a pressure situation. You don't want to do too much, but what you're doing is far too little. You've got to be right there in the middle. Your horse is never going to learn to adapt unless you adapt him."

For the rest of the clinic I watched this woman learn to work with this concept. She was a little tentative at first, then as she *saw results, she grew braver and more adept with her use of Approach and Retreat. The smile on her face grew bigger every time her horse responded and grew more tolerant of the pressure she was creating.*

This lesson illustrates how to use pressure and release of pressure—or *Approach and Retreat*—to access what I see as the three distinct areas of a horse's mind. Picture a horse standing in the middle of a circle. In the space just around him, you have what I call his "comfort zone." Just outside his comfort zone is a space I call his "unsure zone." Everything beyond his unsure zone is what I call his "life-threatening zone" (photos 18.2 A–C).

When you first train a wild horse, say a Mustang, his "comfort zone" is extremely small. A domesticated horse that has been around human beings his whole life, on the other hand, will have a really large "comfort zone." When you first capture a wild Mustang, there are very few things that will keep him in his natural comfort area. Just about anything you do will send him straight into his "unsure zone." If you try to touch him—that's "unsure." You show him the lead rope—that's "unsure."

Now when you put a lot of pressure on that colt—if you introduce really spooky things to him—he will be so frightened that he'll go into the "life-threatening zone." When a horse gets into his "life-threatening zone," he's only focused on survival so he doesn't learn very well.

By using the right amount of pressure and the *Approach and Retreat* method, you can gradually increase a horse's "comfort zone"—or the amount of pressure he will tolerate without reacting. But here's the trick: If you apply too much pressure and a horse gets so panicky and upset that he moves straight through the "unsure zone" to the "life-threatening zone," he can't learn because all he cares about at that point is living through the experience. And, as you saw with the horse in my example, if you apply too little pressure, he doesn't learn to handle anything at all (photos 18.2 A–C).

Your goal, then, is that every single time you put pressure on a horse, you want to get that horse to go to his "unsure zone." Every time he goes there, your job is to keep the pressure on until he finds the answer. Once he finds the right answer, you release the pressure to put him back in his "comfort zone." If you repeat this process every day, then every day the "comfort zone" will get a little bit bigger.

Imagine a little kid in a swimming pool who goes from the shallow end to a little deeper water—and then back to the shallow. Every time

When he's in his "unsure zone," you have an opportunity to desensitize him.

18.2 A–C **When a horse is in his "comfort zone," as this one is, he is able to learn.**

he is able to get back to the shallow end, he feels a little bit braver. Each time he goes a little deeper, he goes back to the shallow end again. Pretty soon he knows he can go all the way into the deep end and then get back to the shallow end safely.

The goal when you're training a horse is to get his "comfort zone" to be really big. If it is huge, then that means your horse is not very frightened, he accepts new things, and he understands how to handle pressure. My horse, Mindy, for example, has a massive "comfort zone." At the other end of the spectrum, a wild Mustang has a tiny one—he is not comfortable with anything I do when I first start training him.

Find the edges

The trick is to learn in each horse you work with where the line is between the "comfort" and the "unsure zone"—and between the "unsure" and the "life-threatening zone." You have to be able to use just enough of the right kind of pressure to get the horse to move across that line, out of his "comfort zone" into his "unsure zone," without frightening him so much that he moves all the way into the "life-threatening zone."

And when he's in his "life-threatening zone," his mind is occupied with fear and his only concern is survival.

How do you do this? Watch your horse's demeanor. You'll be able to see when he is approaching the edge of a zone. Know the five signs of relaxing: licking his lips, cocking a hind leg, lowering his head, blinking his eyes, or taking a deep breath.

A horse in his "unsure zone" is not showing any of these signs. Instead, he is very alert. His expression is watchful, as if to say, "Um, well, I'm not very comfortable with this, but I'm not quite ready to panic yet. I think I'll just wait here a minute and see what else happens before I run."

A horse nearing the edge of his "unsure zone" and entering the "life-threatening zone" is very easy to spot. His eyes get big and wide, his head goes straight up in the air. He snorts and flares his nostrils, the veins in his neck might kind of protrude, his whole body is very tight and tense, and his tail might be clamped down.

He just has that worried or panicked look on his face. His whole expression and demeanor says, "Oh my God! I'm about to be killed!" First, imagine how you'd look at someone if you thought he might hurt you ("unsure"). Then, imagine how you'd look at someone walking toward you with a bloody axe in his hand ("life-threatening"). That's the difference in demeanor and expression you need to watch for.

Enlarging the right area

When a horse does go all the way to the "life-threatening zone," can he ever come back to the "comfort zone"? The answer is yes, but it is important to understand that every time a horse goes into the "life-threatening zone," the chances of him injuring himself, or you, by panicking are very high. For example, he might get so frightened he spins and runs into a tree. Or, he might get so frightened that he kicks at the plastic bag you're holding, but instead of kicking the bag, he kicks you in the face.

You want to make sure that you pressure the horse enough that he goes into his "unsure zone," but not so much that he goes into his "life-threatening zone." This is how you gradually get his "comfort zone" as big as you possibly can.

A good example of this process is when we do my *Lungeing for Respect—Stage Two* exercise. When we first start doing rollbacks with a horse on a lunge line, some horses, especially Thoroughbreds and Arabs, get very nervous and upset about them. They'll start to run around even faster, and they'll actually get worse than when we began.

So what do I do when a horse starts getting nervous? I just keep on turning him and turning him and turning him. After three or four minutes of this, the horse starts to get a little tired, then he starts to relax, and then he starts to turn slower and better. After about 10 more minutes, he handles the pressure really well and is not flustered by it at all. His "comfort zone" has then expanded to include rollbacks on a lunge line.

Now, if I had backed off that pressure when he first started to get nervous and upset, it would have taught him that all he has to do to get out of *Lunging for Respect—Stage Two* is lose his marbles and I'll just pack up my bags and go home. Even though I didn't add a lot more pressure, I continued to stop, turn, stop, turn until the horse probably said to himself, "You know what? This is not going to end. I might as well just slow down a little bit and think about how I'm going to get myself out of this situation."

Hit the road

Another good example of enlarging a horse's "comfort zone" is taking him away from home. Your horse is never going to get comfortable away from home unless you actually take him away. That's why I always take my two-year-olds and three-year-olds away a lot before I ever begin showing them. I want them to get used to going away from the ranch, being tied to a horse trailer all day, listening to the loudspeakers at the horse show, seeing all the kids and people, getting used to streamers, flapping signs, and dogs running around.

When I make the effort to expose them to these experiences when they're young, by the time they're four years old and ready to show, they're used to it all. If I didn't take my horse off the ranch until the day I first went to a horse show, he'd be a complete idiot when I got there. And worse, he would not be focused on me.

How do you expect your kids to behave well at a nice restaurant if you don't ever take them to a nice restaurant? If you always eat at home and then one day you take them to a restaurant, you can't expect them to handle it very well. But if you keep making an effort to take them to restaurants, and you are consistent at praising them when they do well and disciplining them when they make mistakes, eventually they'll figure out that when they go to a restaurant they have to behave themselves.

So if you make the effort to learn how to recognize the edges of your horse's "zones" and be deliberate in your practice of using pressure to move him into his "unsure zone" and releasing it when he finds the right answer, you'll increase his "comfort zone" and have a much less reactive horse.

Lesson 19

It takes time, knowledge, experience— and desire—to get a well-trained horse

Evaluating your abilities, choosing the right kind of horse, and having specific goals will make your horse experience the best it can be.

AN *older man had waited in line for quite a while at one of my tour stops to ask me this question: "Clinton, I've got this 23-year-old broodmare that attacks people and tries to kill them. Can she be retrained?"*

I looked at him for a moment and tried to figure out the best way to phrase my answer. Finally I said, "Sure, she can be retrained." I paused, not sure what his response would be to this next part. "But why would you want to?"

He stood there for a moment, as if searching for a response that would make sense. "Well, I'm kind of attached to her," he said. "I've had her a really long time, and I feel bad that I really haven't ever had the time to do anything with her. Now she's gotten so bad, I have started to wonder if anything can be done with her at all."

Now, I understood that the man was emotionally attached to the horse, and he probably had a variety of reasons why he now wanted to retrain her. I really didn't have an issue with whether he trained this horse or not—that was his own quest and goal.

But my answer to him at that point was, "Okay, then, here's what you need to understand. If it takes 200 hours to get this 23-year-old broodmare to be a safe, respectful, willing horse on the ground and under saddle, it might take you just 40 hours to get any other horse to the same level. So understand that while it can be done, you're going to be spending an extra 160 hours on this problem horse."

"Well, I'm retired now, and I do have the time," he said.

Left:19.1 **When I'm showing potential buyers a horse I have for sale, what I'm really showing them is countless hours of dedicated work and training.**

"And then," I continued, "in addition to time, you'll have to be willing to acquire the knowledge and experience it will take to retrain this horse."

"That's why I'm here," he said.

"That's great," I said. "And it is an excellent start. But before you try these exercises with this particular mare, you need to practice them with other, more respectful horses so you can get good at this method before you work with her. Are you willing to do that?"

"Well, yes," he said, "I do have access to other horses I can work with first to practice."

"Good luck to you, mate," I said. "But remember that you have to be very consistent and work with her at least five days a week. Consistency is your greatest ally—and inconsistency is your greatest enemy."

What this lesson reinforces for me is that to train a horse, you have to have three things—time, knowledge, and experience. Even if you've got the knowledge, if you don't have the time, it's not going to work. And if you have the time, but you don't have the knowledge or experience, it's probably not going to work, either.

In addition to these three things, you've also got to have the personal desire to train a particular horse.

It's not uncommon for people to ask me if they can turn a "bad-minded" horse, like this man's 23-year-old mare, into a safe and willing partner by following my Method. My answer is that it depends. It depends first of all on how much time, knowledge, and experience they have. Then I ask whether this is something they really want to spend their time and energy doing.

It takes a lot of time and consistency to get that kind of horse back on track. You're going to have to dedicate five to six days a week working with a horse like that. And, if she's that difficult, she's not going to turn her attitude around and let you learn on her all at the same time. A bad-minded horse with issues requires someone with knowledge and experience. Beginners need well-broke, respectful horses that already know their job.

Next, you have to ask yourself if it's worth it. For me personally, it's not. In the 200 hours it might take me to retrain a bad-minded horse, I could have spent 50 hours and gotten better results with even an average horse. So it makes a lot more sense to me to start out with a better-minded horse than to fix one with problems.

19.2 **Rather than fix "bad-minded" horses, what I prefer to do now is work with horses that are young, athletic, and talented. It is much more fun for me to train a horse that really wants to do his job than it is to fix one that doesn't.**

Some people, however, choose to work with difficult horses based on emotional reasons or as a challenge, which is fine if you have the experience. I used to love this sort of challenge. As a kid in Australia, I'd seek out the very worst ones I could find in my neighborhood and those were the horses I wanted to train.

And when I first started doing clinics in the United States, I used to advertise that I wanted the worst horse to show up at every tour stop because I loved the challenge of fixing it. But now that I'm a little older— and maybe just a little bit smarter—I don't want to do that anymore. It's just not worth it to me to spend that much time on a horse that won't ever be as good as a horse that is naturally good-minded.

Rather than fixing bad-minded horses, what I prefer to do now is work with young horses that are very talented, physical, and dynamic. It is much more fun to me now to train a horse who wants to do his job (photo 19.2). I suppose this is like being a teacher in a classroom with kids who want to learn, want to be in school, want to excel, and who always do the best they can. These are the kids that are fun to teach.

Kids like this most likely make teaching a very different experience from trying to teach the little brats in the back of the class who don't

19.3 **Should you just get rid of your bad-minded horse? The answer is, "It depends." Do you have the time, knowledge, experience, and desire to fix what's wrong?**

want to be there, never shut up, and are unwilling to cooperate. Working with them is probably a pain in the neck. They have no manners and everything you try to do with them is a constant struggle. It's the same with horses—and it's no wonder that it's more fun to spend more time with the good ones!

Build your confidence, don't wreck it

Does this mean you should just get rid of your difficult horse? Only you can make that decision. What I'm telling you is to seriously consider whether you have the time, knowledge, and experience that it will take to retrain this horse. If the answer is no, then do what's best for you *and* the horse and give him to somebody who does have what it takes to work with him (photo 19.3).

Above all, as I told the man with the 23-year-old mare, don't try to learn my program on a problem horse. Have a horse that will build your confidence, not wreck it. Horses are excellent at making you walk back from the barn on some days thinking you're God's gift to the world—then, the very next day, walk back from the barn with your head lowered and tears rolling down your face. As good as horses are at building up your confidence, they are just as good at wrecking it!

Why do well-trained horses cost so much?

The simple truth is that not only does training horses require time, knowledge, and experience, but to get a horse *well-trained* takes quite a bit of all three. That's why well-trained horses cost so much. Someone has put in a considerable amount of time, knowledge, and experience to get the horse to that level.

People ask me how long it would take to train a horse like my Mindy or Diez. It would take me two years of working with that horse five to six days a week—if he had enough talent and ability—to get him to where Mindy and Diez are. That's two solid years of my being consistent in working with the horse five or six days a week.

The hardest thing to get most people to do is to put enough time and repetition into their horses. There are really only three ways to get a horse trained: buy a well-trained horse; train it yourself; or pay someone else to train it (photos 19.4 A–C). And even if you buy a horse already well trained or pay to have him trained, you've still got to be willing to *maintain* that training with some degree of consistent work.

Horses don't train themselves—or even maintain their training—in the stall or pasture, just as children don't educate themselves by sitting in front of the TV. For a horse to get—and stay—well trained, you have to be willing to spend time working with him. You have to do just what you do with your children in order to teach them what they need to know and how to behave.

So whether you buy your horse trained, train it yourself, or pay someone else to train it, a well-trained horse represents a lot of time and/or money. We sell my Signature Horses for anywhere from $20,000 to $25,000. These are horses that are safe, quiet, and extremely good on the trail and in the arena. They know my entire horsemanship program. People pay this price not because they are exceptionally well-bred or extremely talented, but because we have spent at least a year—some-

19.4 A–C **There are only three ways to get a well-trained horse: Buy it trained; pay someone to train it; or train it yourself. Here I am explaining to this prospective buyer how this horse has been trained through my Method to be soft and supple in all five body parts, and to be quiet, respectful, and responsive.**

The decision to buy a well-trained horse is only part of the equation. You have to be willing to learn how to maintain that training and ride that horse consistently to keep his training at that level.

Remember: "Horses are nothing more than maintenance with legs!"

times closer to two years—training these horses to do everything.

What people are buying is the fact that my apprentices and I have spent a lot of time teaching them to be safe, willing, dependable mounts. They're paying for the luxury that *they* didn't have to spend that kind of time with the horse, and they didn't have to put the horse in training and gamble whether or not it would turn out to be suitable.

When people come to the ranch to ride one of our Signature Horses, they get to take the horse outside, ride him on the trail, and haul him away and ride him in different environments to see how he reacts to new surroundings and to being away from home. When someone buys one of these horses, they're buying the guarantee that this horse will work for them and keep them safe.

But remember, even if you buy a well-trained horse, he will still require some maintenance to *keep* performing well. You're not going to be able to give him a couple of months off and then just go saddle him up, get on him, and expect him not to be a little fresh and feeling his oats. You're going to need to lunge him, do some groundwork, and get him using the thinking side of his brain before you ride him.

I wish we could sell horses to people with a stamp or a guarantee that if he's this good now, he will always be this good, but we can't.

Even a brand new car requires some maintenance. Cars don't stay new forever, and they need regular, consistent maintenance to stay in good working order. Unlike a car, a horse is a living creature with emotions, moods, good days and bad days. All horses require maintenance— they're nothing more than maintenance with legs, remember?

Some horses only need a little maintenance, and some need a lot. The amount each horse requires really depends on how well the horse is trained and how bad his habits were before you got him. The most important thing to understand here is that horses never stay the same. Every single day a horse will either get a little better or a little worse, but one thing is for sure: he will never just stay the same.

When you learn how to match your time, knowledge and experience to a horse that you will enjoy training for *whatever* reason, you'll most likely find that you can achieve and maintain the very best that horse has to give. Believe me, mate, it is a commitment that is well worth the effort.

Lesson 20

Success is just around the corner—the trouble is, most people quit before they reach the corner!

Achieving success in horse training often comes down to patience, persistence, and consistency — even when it seems like the horse is never going to understand.

THE *horse I was riding for Gordon was really stiff and sorry. He didn't want to give his face vertically or laterally. I started out doing a little bit of lateral flexion. I did it for a couple of days and he made some improvement, but then I didn't worry about doing it anymore.*

Next, I started working on trying to get his head down on his sliding stops and backing, trying to get more vertical flexion out of him. For the next week, every day I rode him he got worse and worse, stiffer and stiffer.

I was trying to get his head down tucked in vertically, but the problem was, I didn't have him soft laterally first. When I asked Gordon about it, Gordon said, "Go back and do more lateral flexion. For the next seven days straight, do nothing more than lateral flexion."

So that's what I did—nothing but lateral flexion on this horse for the next seven days. One-Rein Stops at the walk, trot, and canter—hundreds and hundreds of lateral flexions every single day. At the end of the week I was amazed at how soft this horse was when I went back to asking him to give his face vertically, stop, and back up.

This experience illustrates one of the most important lessons I learned from Gordon McKinlay. Gordon is a typical Capricorn—always climbing that mountain. He may not be very fast, he may not be all that nimble, but he just keeps on climbing, step-by-step, until he gets to the top.

Left: 20.1 **When you start teaching a horse something new, it's not usually pretty at first. A good example of this is when you first ask a horse to flex and give to the halter and lead rope. Most horses will resist, as this one is.**

With horse training, what this means is that you have to keep going, step-by-step, until you reach your goal. The surprising thing about training horses is that often, right when you think something is not *ever* going to work, the next thing you know, it does!

What I've found is that most people quit far too early. They want results in the first two minutes, and when it doesn't happen, they never even realize that they were just around the corner from success.

Basically, horse training amounts to putting your horse into a series of binds and letting him figure his own way out of them. I compare this to putting a horse into a giant stall with eight doors. If he tries all eight doors and only the last one opens, the next time you put him in there, he'll still try them all before finding the right one. Then next time, he may try only a few before he remembers which one is the right door. Within a few more days, he'll eventually go straight to the right door. But his mind has to go through that process of discovering the right answer.

If you are not patient and persistent enough to wait it out until your horse finds the right answer, the success you are looking for will keep eluding you.

Another example of this bind is when you pick up the lead rope to ask a horse to flex for the very first time. You pick it up, you apply pressure to the lead rope and the halter and it makes the horse feel uncomfortable. You've put him in somewhat of a bind. His job now is to figure a way out of the bind, which in this case, of course, is to stop moving his feet and bend his head and neck to create a little slack in the lead rope. Your responsibility at this point is to *wait* until he finds that answer—and then release the lead rope immediately to give him the reward that tells him he got it.

Remember, horses learn from the *release* of pressure—not from the pressure itself.

When many people try to bend the horse's head and neck for the first time, they want that horse to immediately "give." You've got to wait it out. Some horses may take a minute, while others may stand there for 10 minutes before they "give." Some horses may run all over the pen to try to get away from that pressure.

Regardless of what a horse does, you have to wait it out. Because, again, horses are professional people trainers; they are always trying to train people to take the pressure away too early. When you quit too early, you deny your horse the opportunity to find the right answer.

As I keep saying, horses are a lot like children. When you first show a child how to spell his name, you don't just show him once and figure that he's got it. You show him again and again and again. You go over it every day until he can do it on his own. The way he learns how to do it on his own is by repeating the process that allows him to find the right answer through trial and error.

Repetition is your biggest ally

Two of my exercises where I see people quitting too early are *Flexing the Horse's Head and Neck* and *One-Rein Stops*. Most people want to just flex their horse two or three times on each side and be done with it. Flexing is the key to getting your horse soft, supple, relaxed, and giving to pressure really well. However, for flexing to really work, you've got to do it over and over again. To get your horse to understand when you are first trying to flex, repetition is your greatest ally.

As a general rule when I begin to get a horse soft and supple laterally—say for the initial 10 to 14 rides after the "concept lesson," every day I'm going to spend 10 minutes at the standstill doing lateral flexion, 10 minutes at walk doing *One-Rein Stops*, 10 minutes at the trot doing *One-Rein Stops*, and 10 minutes at the canter doing *One-Rein Stops*. People ask, "Clinton, do you mean to say that you'll actually spend 40 minutes, 14 days straight, doing nothing but lateral flexion?"

My response is, "That's correct!" I'm going to do that until my horse is absolutely feather light and all it takes is one finger to soften that horse up. That's because I understand the importance of getting a horse that soft and supple laterally.

As Gordon's amazing lesson demonstrated to me in a way I have never forgotten, lateral flexion is not something you just do once or twice. When you practice flexing until it becomes effortless for both you and your horse, you'll probably also find that most of your vertical flexion work has been done for you!

Don't stop *Sending* before you get there

My *Sending* exercise is another area where I often see people quitting far too soon. In this exercise, you direct your horse through a space you create between yourself and a fence or object, into or out of the stall, over a puddle or gully, or through some other tight, narrow space.

When you first start this exercise, most horses want to hurry through the "gap." What you've got to do is be patient and persistent and

20.2 A–C **In the beginning with the Sending exercise, horses want to hurry—or even jump—through the space.**

Just be patient and persistent and keep Sending him back and forth until he starts to use the "thinking" side of his brain. You'll know this is happening when he slows down, starts to relax, and moves through the space calmly. If you stop the Sending exercise before this happens, you haven't accomplished anything at all.

My horse has discovered that the spooky blue tarp is no threat at all, and to reinforce this, I let him rest and get his air back while standing on it.

keep *Sending* them back and forth until they start using the thinking side of their brain, start to relax, and come through very calmly, either at a walk or at a slow jog. That's the reaction you're looking for, and if you stop *Sending* before you get there, you haven't accomplished anything at all (photos 20.2 A–C).

You're not looking for the horse to sprint through the gap, jump over the log, or panic through the tight, narrow space. That's what a horse wants to do naturally—that's the "reacting" side of his brain talking. You have to keep working him, moving his feet through all that reactivity until he calms down and starts using the "thinking" side of his brain.

Now, once the horse *is* using the thinking side of his brain and coming through calmly, don't repeat this exercise a thousand more times. Once he gets it right, move on to something else. You may want to come back and check on this exercise from time to time during the next few days, but you're not going to drill it for hours. Once the horse gets it, reward him and move on.

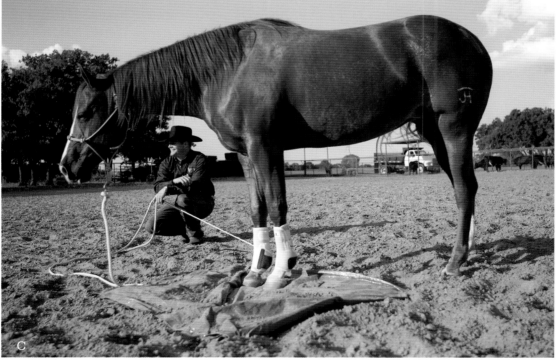

True relaxation is well worth the wait

Another place where I see people quitting too early is while waiting for their horse to relax. There are five major signs of a horse relaxing: the horse lowers his head and neck; licks his lips; cocks a hind leg; takes a deep breath; or blinks his eyes.

There are other signs of relaxation, too, such as shaking his whole body like a dog, rolling on the ground, and a few others, but most people are not conscious of any of these signs, and even if they are, they're not patient enough to wait for the horse to show them.

Desensitizing your horse to spooky objects

I want my horse to be desensitized to as many objects as possible. What is an "object"? An object is anything that is new or unfamiliar to him. If something lives in his stall or pasture, a horse is not frightened of it because he has spent so much time around it that he has automatically become desensitized.

Horses especially hate objects that move and make noise. A good example of one of the things horses hate most is the plastic bag: it's an *object* that both *moves* AND *makes noise*—a triple bad deal (photo 20.3)!

Horses by nature are relatively easy to desensitize because they're programmed that way. If horses were hard to desensitize, they'd never survive in the wild because every time something moved they'd start running. They'd never have time to eat, sleep, or reproduce. Horses in the wild have to be able to quickly figure out what they need to run away from, such as a predator, and what they need to ignore, such as tree branches moving in the wind.

When you're desensitizing a horse to spooky objects, it is very important that you keep the stimulus present and wait for two things to happen. You first wait for the horse's feet to stop moving. Mother Nature has told him that when he gets frightened he needs to run away from danger. What we want to teach the horse is that when he gets frightened, he needs to instead just stand still and fall asleep to make the scary object go away.

So if you walk toward your horse with a dreaded plastic bag, and you have his head tipped toward you, when he goes to run away, he'll just run in a circle with his head facing you. If you just hold the plastic bag there, his feet will eventually stop moving and he'll stand still. That's

20.3 **Horses hate unusual objects, and a plastic bag is one of those horses hate the most because it is an object that moves AND makes noise—a triple bad deal! I'm teaching this horse to ignore the stimulus of a noisy moving object. It is important to keep the pressure on until the horse stands still and gives you one of the five signs of relaxation (see p. 166). If you quit too soon, you're only teaching him to react!**

the first thing he has to do: acknowledge that running away is not the right answer.

The second thing I'm going to wait for before I take the plastic bag away is for him to show me one of those five signs of relaxation. Once he has shown me one of these signs (sometimes he'll show more than one) I'll retreat—take the plastic bag away—and rub the horse with my hand.

There are some horses out there, however, that might stand still, but won't show one of the other physical signs of relaxing. In that case, I just wait 15 seconds and then retreat. It's a little bit of "What happens first?" If a horse stands still for 15 seconds and doesn't move his feet, but doesn't show another sign of relaxing, I'll still retreat.

A lot of people will just wait until the horse stands still, and then they take the pressure away. And a lot of horses will trick you—just because he stands still doesn't mean he's truly relaxed. This is where you just have to use your judgment, which will get better the more you practice. Just remember: If you take the pressure away when your horse is still thinking about running, or while he's still very nervous, you reward him for being nervous and thinking that running is the right answer.

Remember, horses don't learn from pressure, but from the release of pressure. Let your horse tell you when you need to take the pressure away.

When desensitizing, I have a little rule of thumb: You can never do it too long. You can quit too early, but you can almost never do it too long. So if you are ever in doubt as to whether you should stop or keep going, my recommendation is to always keep going. It never hurts to go a few extra seconds, but it certainly could hurt if you quit too early.

Reward the right moves

The same thing goes for sensitizing your horse to pressure. When a lot of people ask their horse to lunge to the left, they point with their left hand and twirl their Handy Stick and String up toward the horse's neck. If the horse backs up instead of turning left, they often take the pressure of the Handy Stick and String away. All that does is reward the horse for backing up.

If my horse backs up instead of moving left as I ask, what I do then is run more toward him, continuing to twirl that Handy Stick and String—in other words keep applying that pressure—and wait for the horse to turn left and go forward. When he does turn left and starts moving forward, I immediately stop moving the Handy Stick and String to take that pressure away.

People have a tendency when they're sensitizing—getting the horse's feet to move—that whenever the horse's feet move, even if it's not in the direction they want the feet to move, they take the pressure off. They think that taking the pressure away with any movement is the right thing to do, but on the contrary: If the horse is moving the wrong way you are just rewarding the *wrong kind* of movement.

The first time you ask a horse to go left, he might back up, he might run sideways, he might rear, or he might stand there and ignore you. It doesn't matter what the horse is doing. If it's not what you want—or at least in the direction you want—don't take away the pressure. Don't make the horse move away from you, make it uncomfortable for him *not* to move away from you. By doing this, through repetition, he'll quickly figure out that backing *is not* the right answer—and that turning left and going forward *is* the right answer.

Although we used lunging here as the example, this pretty much applies to anything. *Do not take the pressure away until the horse moves his feet in the direction you want.* It may not be the perfect circle to the left, and he may not do it exactly how you want, but you've got to reward any sort of a try where he moves his feet *in that direction.* After enough repetition of this, the horse will figure out that when you point your hand to the left and pick up the Handy Stick, he'd better immediately start to lunge in that direction to avoid the pressure.

As I mentioned in an earlier lesson, I find that most adults do a pretty good job of sensitizing their horses, but they do a poor job of desensitizing. Adults go out of their way not to do anything that might spook or scare the horse.

Children, on the other hand—especially little children—do a really good job of desensitizing their horses and ponies. Kids are always hanging off their horse, grabbing his ears, pulling on his tail, climbing all over his back like an army of ants. They do this over and over and over again until their horse just ignores it.

Oddly enough, with horses, the less you try to scare them, the spookier they get. I know it may not sound right, but the more you try to spook or scare a horse, the calmer and quieter and less spooky he will get. That is hard for most people to believe, but it's the truth. The key is when you do try to scare your horse, you have to keep going until he starts to use the thinking side of his brain, stops his feet, and shows you one or more of those five signs of relaxing.

A slow lope is no accident

Perhaps the biggest area where I see people quitting far too early is when loping. Say you want your horse to lope slowly, like Mindy and Diez do on my DVDs, on a big loose rein, relaxed and quiet, with a slow, consistent beat. The only way I know to get a horse to do that is to put some steady miles under his feet (photo 20.4).

For a horse to get good at loping, you have to give him enough chances to practice it. You've got to lope him and lope him and lope him. And when he is really tired, you've got to lope him some more. And just when your horse thinks he is going to die if he goes another step, what do you do? You lope him some more!

I exaggerate this point a little bit here because most people lope their horse for about four minutes and then say, "Oh my goodness, he's

tired, I need to quit." What this really means is "*I'm* tired and *I* need to quit." The horse is just getting started. It is very important to stay with the horse until he is *begging* to slow down.

When you first start cantering a young horse and you want him to go, say, 15 miles per hour, he might start out going 18 miles per hour. Just stay with him for the first 5 to 10 minutes until he backs down to the speed you want.

Keep in mind that he's probably not going to go as slowly as you'd like in the first few sessions, but keep loping until you feel like he wants to slow down. If he's still acting like "This is fun! Yippee! Let's get out of here!" He's telling you that you haven't put enough miles under his feet.

That's why I say that sometimes you have to "go through a horse's lungs to get to his feet." That means that you have to take away his air to get his feet to do what you want them to—and then his feet get back to his brain, which is ultimately what you want. You want a horse to *want* to lope slowly whether he's fresh or tired. In the beginning, though, you may have to make him physically tired to give him that desire.

Although this is true for the majority of horses, there are some out there, especially the more hot-blooded breeds like Thoroughbreds and Arabs, that just want to go, go, go. The longer you lope them, the faster they get. They just get faster and faster and sillier and sillier. Letting those horses lope forever will not work, because the more they get out of air, the more panicked they get.

To get that kind of horse to slow down, you have to also make them think. You do that with lots of transitions, especially bending transitions. Do a *One-Rein Stop* and trot the horse off. Bend him around, let him walk two or three circles, lope him off for four or five strides; then bend him around, let him walk two or three circles, and lope him off again. By doing a lot of bending, transitions, and *One-Rein Stops*, you keep his mind busy and engaged—and distracted from wanting to run.

The secret is not to go too far between transitions. For example, if I'm cantering, I don't let him go more than five strides before I go into a

20.4 **One thing I've noticed is that most people quit too soon when loping their horse. To teach your horse to lope slowly and calmly as my reining horse, Sparkles, is doing here, lope him until you think he wants to stop. Then, lope him some more. When you feel that he is begging to stop, what do you do? Lope him some more! This is what builds his conditioning—mentally and physically—so he is able to lope calmly until you tell him to do something else.**

downward transition. The longer you let him lope, the more he will start to ignore you and want to run.

I lope my two-year-olds a lot. Teaching a horse to lope slowly is the most important thing you can teach a two-year-old because it sets up a foundation for the rest of his life. If your horse is green at loping and not very good at it, if he goes too fast or is difficult to ride and you've never learned how to canter before, he's not going to be a good horse for you to learn and build your confidence on. You need to find a horse that automatically wants to lope slowly and be quiet and soft so you can build on that.

I have a saying: "Green horse plus green rider is a recipe for disaster." To help you build your confidence and learn to canter when you own a green horse, borrow a friend's horse for a couple of weeks or lease a horse for 30 days. Many people wreck their confidence by trying to learn to canter on a horse that isn't confident cantering himself. When the rider is not confident and the horse is not confident, they just beat up on each other's lack of confidence.

Remember when you got your first bike? You probably had training wheels and big, wide tires. When you first got on, you probably didn't have very good balance, you didn't stop very well, and you weren't very consistent in your turns. Sometimes you'd go too fast, and you didn't have good rhythm or balance. So how did you develop really good rhythm and balance on a bicycle? You rode it and you rode it and you rode it. Someone probably had to practically beat you with a stick to make you get off it. Most likely, you pretty much wore the tires out because it was fun, it was new, and it was something you wanted.

That's exactly how horses are with loping. If you want your horse to get good at it, give him a chance to ride his new bike. Give him a chance to get comfortable and balanced. When you first start loping a young horse, he won't know things like how fast to go, or what lead to be on. He'll probably lope too fast, drop to a trot, spook away from objects, and have a lack of consistency in his gait.

When I first start loping a two-year-old or even an older horse with problems, I don't care what lead he's on. I don't care where his head is. I don't care if he drops his shoulder. What I care about is if he travels on a loose rein and stays at that gait consistently. When I feel him wanting to go slower, I lope him for a few more minutes. When he's *begging* to go slower, that's when I'll let him come to a stop.

When I do decide to let him stop, I'll usually stop him in the middle of the arena, or if there's one particular end or area of the arena he is scared of, I'll go there to let him rest so that he'll learn that it is not a bad place, but rather, a *good* area where he can go to get his air back. When your horse is hooked on the gate, don't rest him anywhere near it, but at the opposite end of the arena. Then he will not be so anxious to get back to the gate.

Just remember, mate, whatever you're trying to teach your horse, just be patient, stay with it, and use pressure and the five signs of relaxation to get all the way to the corner—because success is waiting for you just around it. All you have to do is take those few extra steps around the corner to find the success you're looking for.

Index